Color Me Healthy Wealthy And Wise

Transform Your Life with Colors & Crystals

Carolyn White PhD

Copyright © 2016 Carolyn White PhD. All rights reserved. No portion of this book may be reproduced mechanically, electronically, or by any other means, including photocopying, without written permission of the author and publisher. It is illegal to copy this book, post it to a website, or distribute it by any other means without permission from the author and Publisher.
Carolyn White PhD

www.CarolynWhitePhD.com

www.ChakraCoach.me

ISBN-13:978-0692632567
ISBN-10:0692632565

Limits of Liability and Disclaimer of Warranty
The author and publisher shall not be liable for your misuse of this material. This book is strictly for informational and educational purposes.

Warning – Disclaimer
The purpose of this book is to educate and entertain. The author and/or publisher do not guarantee that anyone following these techniques, suggestions, tips, ideas, or strategies will become successful.
The author and/or publisher shall have neither liability nor responsibility to anyone with respect to any loss or damage caused, or alleged to be caused, directly or indirectly by the information contained in this book.

Cover and Interior Illustrations: Carolyn White

Dedication

To all my mentors—past, present and future: Thank you for sharing your knowledge, wisdom and love!

To my wonderful loving husband Gerry, who spent many hours proofreading and being the "sounding board" for ideas.
Thank you for being here for me.

To you, my dear reader, I dedicate my words to you:

Let my sense of presence flow from Mother Earth.

Let my wisdom and knowledge flow from Spirit.

Let my words flow from my Heart.

Be color-full! Be joyful! Be blessed! Be You!

Learn more from Carolyn White PhD

Want to learn more about your Human Energy System—your Aura and Chakras? Invite us to your party or special event. Host an Aura Photography and Chakra Imaging private party in the comfort of your own home or venue. Unique and fantastic fun! Discover your True Colors and learn more about your Human Energy System.

Each guest receives their individual aura photo and chakra image, a hand-out briefly explaining the colors and the chakras, plus a personal interpretation by Dr. Carolyn.

Inspiring—Educational—Entertaining

➢Personal in-depth readings and coaching offered by appointment.

➢Available for speaking engagements and group classes.

Contact Gerry or Carolyn White at www.ChakraCoach.me for more information.

Other Books by Carolyn White PhD

Chakra Mastery: 7 Keys to Discover Your Inner Wisdom (2015)

Chakra Mastery Journal Series

Think It->Say It->Be It: Use Your Words to Change Your Life (2013)

Co-Author:

The Gratitude Project: Celebrating 365 Days of Gratitude (2014)

5 Secrets to Balanced Healthy Living: The Power of the Five Elements (2013)

Your Soaring Phoenix: Profound Tools for Spiritual Ascension With 26 Spiritual Teachers (May 2014)

About the Author

Carolyn White, PhD, is a chakra life coach, author, speaker, teacher and metaphysician. As a Certified Aura Video Station consultant, she has helped many individuals understand their Human Energy System—the aura and chakras.

Carolyn is the author of *Think It->Say It -> Be It: Use Your Words to Change Your Life, Chakra Mastery: 7 Keys to Discover Your Inner Wisdom* and eight companion journals for *Chakra Mastery*. She has co-authored several books, including *The Gratitude Book Project: Celebrating 365 Days of Gratitude* and *5 Secrets to Balance, Healthy Living: Harnessing to Power of the 5 Elements*.

Carolyn's passion for learning about our Human Energy System (HES) and the Mind/Body/Spirit connection spans over four decades. As a result of her pursuit, Carolyn is a Doctor of Clinical Hypnotherapy (DCH), a Certified Spiritual Counselor (CSC), and an International Hypnosis Federation Certified Instructor (CHI). She is also a Reiki Master and Reflexologist. She has certifications in Neuro-linguistic Programming (NLP), Timeline Therapy and Color Therapy. In 2007, Carolyn completed a doctoral program that awarded her a PhD in Esoteric Studies from American Pacific University.

According to Carolyn, all energy therapies need to be practical and practiced. Her teaching focuses on employing the three H's - Head, Hands, and Heart – as the basic tools of Energy Medicine. Her personal journey after a serious motor vehicle accident in 2008 reaffirmed the healing power of energy medicine.

Carolyn's play shops on Auras and Chakras focus on empowering the individual to discover their inner wisdom while learning about their human energy system.

Besides appearing at holistic fairs and conferences with Aura and Chakra Imaging, Carolyn is a vocalist and bassist, performing with her husband Gerry at various venues.

Contents

Introduction	1
Color Consciousness	3
What is Color?	13
Working with Color	27
How to Work with Color Every day	31
Colors for Children	37
Changing the Energy Within	41
Crystal Magic	49
Crystals and Gemstone Shapes	55
How Do I Know What Crystals To Use?	65
Selecting Programming and Using Crystals	71
Balancing the 7 Major Chakras	79
Putting It All Together	87
The Chakras	95
Archetypal Color Energies	105
Gemstone Correspondences And Guides	125

REFERENCES AND TABLES

ELECTROMAGNETIC SPECTRUM	14
PRIMARIES OF LIGHT	17
PRIMARIES OF PIGMENTS	19
SEVEN SPECTRAL COLORS WHEEL	21
SUBTRACTIVE PIGMENT COLOR WHEEL	23
HUE/TINT/TONE/SHADE COLOR WHEELS	24
"THINK COLOR" ATTRIBUTES	34
COLOR AFFIRMATIONS	44
QUICK ENERGIZER WITH CRYSTALS	76
QUICK TIPS FOR SUCCESS	93
YOUR CHAKRAS/ENERGY CENTERS KEY ASPECTS	96
HIGHER/LOWER OCTAVES OF CHAKRAS	97
ARCHETYPAL ENERGIES OF SEVEN SPECTRAL COLORS	106
REFERENCE TABLES FOR SPECIFIC COLOR APPLICATIONS	110
CHAKRA GEMSTONE CORRESPONDENCES GUIDE	126
GEMSTONE CORRESPONDING ENERGIES	128

Introduction

When I first started writing *Chakra Mastery: 7 Keys to Discover Your Inner Wisdom*, my outline included sections on color and crystals. I believe both play an important part in clearing, balancing and transforming the human energy system (HES).

After covering the basics of the HES and each chakra, I realized the information about colors and crystals as relating to the chakras demanded a separate book. I wanted to share the benefits of color and bring awareness of its impact on the HES.

"Is This Stuff Real, or Just a Bunch of Woo-woo?"

I'm often asked this question when doing aura and chakra imaging. "What's the big deal with color and can using it really do all this stuff?"

If the longevity of a practice validates its proven effectiveness, then using color has been around for a long time. Since early times, color has played an important role in humankind's health, healing and evolution. Even today, color psychology has advanced as a sophisticated tool to stimulate sales and motivate positive behavior.

If color psychology is employed by marketers to influence your buying decisions and behavior, then why don't you use the same strategies to influence your behavior and life?

The same goes for crystals. Over the years of visually observing their interaction with the aura and chakras, I can unequivocally say these gifts from Mother Nature impact the HES. The degree of influence varies from person to person. Rarely do I see an individual with minimal or no response. Often, the effect is noticeable. At times, introducing a crystal into the HES is dramatic. Most of the time, the crystal has a life-affirming influence on the HES. Sometimes, I advise the individual that their HES and the crystal are not resonating with each other and best to stop using that crystal.

Many of us have DNA or past life memories of working with crystals, which is perhaps why you are attracted to them. Edgar Cayce's readings describe the healing temples of Atlantis filled with crystals hanging like stalactites from the ceilings. Legend relates crystal headbands augmented mental awareness and amplified the senses of the Lemurians.

In the chronicles of ancient history, crystals and gemstones served as tools of healing, prophecy and spiritual transformation. From practical applications—Japanese embroiderers held stones to cool their hands so perspiration wouldn't spoil their work—to the crystal capstone of the Great Pyramid at Giza—crystals and gemstones are interwoven into the fabric of humanity.

Why Healthy, Wealthy and Wise?

Good health is probably your most important asset. Learning about color and crystals assists you in achieving the optimal health of your body, mind and spirit.

Money is only one layer of the wealth onion. By definition, wealthy includes having abundant resources or assets at your disposal. From a purely economics perspective, to quote Adam Smith, "The Wealth of a Nation was not in the accumulation of commodities nor in the resource reserves that a nation may happen to possess. But rather wealth exists in the productive knowledge of its people."[1]

Learning about color and crystals and knowing how to use these assets become powerful resources for your life.

Application of knowledge is experience, which leads to wisdom –– your inner wisdom.

Know thyself —go forth and be color-full!

---

[1] http://www.digitaleconomist.org/wth_4020.html

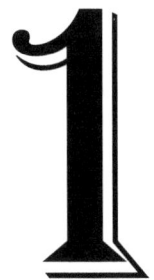

COLOR CONSCIOUSNESS

"Everything is energy and that's all there is to it. Match the frequency of the reality you want and you cannot help but get that reality. It can be no other way. This is not philosophy. This is physics." ~ Albert Einstein

Color Consciousness

In my book, *Chakra Mastery: 7 Keys to Discover Your Inner Wisdom*, I detail how each chakra vibrates at a specified range of frequencies, which are harmonics of the seven spectral colors, i.e. colors of the rainbow when light passes through a prism. Each chakra is therefore represented by a specific color.

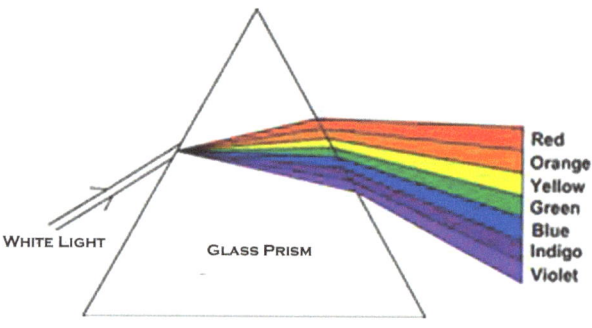

One of the easiest ways to work with the chakras is to bring in the energy of specific colors associated with each. Color is powerful as it expresses light.

Why is color so important when working with the chakras? Color is the most generally and broadly available modality. It is readily at hand as you live, breathe, work and play in a sea of color. Color surrounds you and you can choose what colors to have in your environment via clothing, décor, everyday accessories and tools.

Color is probably the most economical and practical way to balance energy as it is interwoven throughout our environment. Unless required by a job, you have choices as to what colors to wear. Even if you spend the day in a uniform, you can don colorful undergarments and perhaps wear jewelry with a certain gemstone or color.

You have choices as to what colors surround your living space. Even if you live in a rental and can't paint the walls, you can still bring color into your life through accessories such as towels, kitchen appliances and utensils, bed linens, personal grooming accessories and decorating accents. When you are aware of the power of color, you realize the necessity of including certain colors into your life and, hence, your human energy field.

Color influences human emotions as it bypasses the logical, reasoning mind and speaks to the subconscious mind. If you hear a sound, it may or may not evoke a corresponding thought or emotion. Yet, viewing a color probably arouses at least one feeling or thought. Consider, what do you experience when you see the color red? Stop as in a stop sign? Passion? Anger? Blood? All the aforementioned? None of the above?

This subconscious association between color and our thoughts and emotions led to the development of the science of color psychology. Think about your favorite restaurant—the one you frequent for the ultimate dining experience. Have you ever wondered why McDonald's fixtures started out as primarily red and yellow? Red stimulates the appetite—think about those red checkered table cloths that invite you to dine in an Italian restaurant. Yellow makes you feel "Happy" (Happy Meal, Ronald McDonald) while subliminally encouraging you to eat and get out quickly. Since 2012, McDonald's chain has been upgrading their décor to more tans and browns, ostensibly to attract a more "upscale" clientele. By 2015, this major fast food chain is experiencing diminishing profits. Besides a growing awareness of food choices and quality, their move from the colors originally bringing success may have contributed to their lagging sales.

Where do associations between colors and chakras originate? How do crystals relate to the chakras and colors? Why is it necessary to understand how correspondences function to work with your chakras, colors and crystals?

"As above, so below; as below so above." ~ Law of Correspondence—Second Law of Hermetic Wisdom

On the surface, the Law of Correspondence seems rather general—as in the heavens, so as in the Earth. This second law of Hermetic wisdom relies on the principle of resonant frequencies. Correspondences occur when similar ideas, thought forms or physical objects vibrate at resonant frequencies and entrain.

Understanding this concept helps when working with energy, as you are able to attract and change by evoking corresponding thoughts or objects. As well, if you experience challenges in a certain area of your life, you can look to associated energies, which may assist in resolving the problem.

In energy work, a group of corresponding energies are referred to as archetypes. When counseling clients, I remind them the seven major chakras each represents an archetypal energy. As well, colors express archetypal energies.

What is an archetype? By definition, an archetype is the original form or prototype. In the psychology of C. G. Jung an archetype is an inherited idea or mode of thought derived from the experience of the human race and is present in the subconscious of the individual.

Archetypes have been present in societies for millennia. The Ancients, in their wisdom, sought to comprehend the Universe in a language of myth and metaphor. Gods and goddesses carried a range of human attributes, from noble to base. The primary intent of the gods and goddesses was to teach and explain the nature of the cosmos and humanity's relationship to it. The gods and goddesses personified archetypal energies and were never intended as objects of idolatry. No one god or goddess was more important than the other as all emanated from the One Source of Creation and functioned as an integrated system.

When you want to communicate about a mystical experience, you need a common frame of reference. A level of information exchange is necessary that will appeal to the three minds—subconscious, conscious and superconscious (higher self). Color, or hue, and its breadth of properties, such as tint, shade and saturation expresses the gamut of emotional, logical and subconscious communications.

Color is a frame of reference for understanding the archetypal energies of the chakras. A color is a range of frequencies within visible light of the electromagnetic spectrum, which attracts and holds certain archetypal emotions and ideas. All information is contained in light to create life—light is life. Since color is an aspect of light, each range of frequency holds much information.

Consider how color impacts your daily life. What does it mean when you see a red octagon or a yellow inverted triangle street sign? Why it is someone can have the blues yet "true blue" means loyalty? What comes to mind when someone mentions the "red light district?" Why does green indicate "go" on a stop light as well as indicate a state of envy?

Color carries messages to all three minds—conscious, subconscious and superconscious. It often communicates non-verbally to your subconscious mind, evoking emotions (envy) and giving directions (stop/yield). Soft, pastel colors such as pink, peach and lilac suggest tranquil, angelic feelings that connect you with the spiritual.

Often, color messages carry a cultural context. White is universally associated with purity and spirituality. Traditionally, a wedding in Western culture dresses the bride in white, a symbol of her "purity." Yet Oriental cultures reserve white for funerals and red for weddings.

Social mores can throw a myopic view on color, forgetting color is actually a range of frequencies. One of my aura and chakra imaging clients presented a beautifully integrated red aura and well-balanced chakras. The first question from this lady, in her sixties, was, "doesn't red mean a lot of anger?" I explained to her that red holds a range of energetic meaning. After determining from her chakras and talking to her that anger wasn't an issue, we talked about passion. She loved life, was physically fit and enjoyed physical activities—all life qualities she resonated with. I did counsel her that, sometimes, her desire to have issues resolved quickly might lead to impatience—which also struck a chord—and she is a person of action.

When our session completed, my client's cultural bias around red expanded to an understanding of the gamut and possibilities in this color. Her concept of "red" went from one-dimensional to multi-dimensional. Yes, she did admit to minor issues with anger, now realizing this emotion often arose from impatience with others.

Color Works

Color helps you tune into frequency of universal archetypes. Each chakra represents a range of energies in a color wavelength. Since light can contain infinite information, it is one of the best storage, transformation, transportation and delivery systems for archetypal energy.

Chakra/Color Wavelength Values

Between: (A=1 Angstrom -> 10^{-10} Meter)

4460A	3900A	Crown	Violet
4640A	4460A	3rd Eye	Indigo
5000A	4640A	Throat	Blue
5780A	5000A	Heart	Green
5920A	5780A	Solar Plexus	Yellow
6200A	5920A	Sacral	Orange
7800A	6200A	Root	Red

How do the frequencies of light, as expressed in color ranges, correspond to the chakras? The first three chakras—root, sacral and solar plexus—focus on the physical structure of your life. Red, orange and yellow—the colors relating to the root, sacral and solar plexus chakras respectively—are regarded as "warm" in the world of color properties.

As you travel up your body, the chakras—heart, throat, third eye and crown—are associated with increasingly spiritual concerns. The green of the heart chakra is considered a balancing color as this color's frequency ranges from warm yellow-green to cool blue-green.

Blue, indigo and violet are considered cool and "electric," or etheric, colors. The throat, third eye and crown chakras help you connect with the spiritual facets of your life.

Each chakra vibrates at a frequency commensurate with their function. The lower chakras vibrate at a slower rate while the more etheric chakras vibrate at a higher rate. The slower the vibration, the denser the form, which is why it's natural for the three lower chakras—root, sacral and solar plexus—to be involved with denser, more physical aspects of your life.

The chakras' energy patterns emit colors corresponding to their resonant light wave frequencies. This follows the theory of resonance and entrainment as discussed in *Chakra Mastery*. If something vibrates at a certain frequency, it will attract that frequency or a harmonic of that frequency. Valerie Hunt's research at UCLA confirms this phenomenon. Since red is the slowest light wave frequency, it corresponds to the root chakra. The slightly faster frequency of orange is associated with the sacral chakra. As you go up the body, the light wave frequencies mirror their increasing vibratory rate in the corresponding chakra. The fastest light wave frequency, violet, resonates with the crown chakra.

I realize some clairvoyant individuals may dispute this rainbow color/chakra correspondence as it doesn't match their model. Jack Schwartz "saw" the colors for each chakra as root/red orange; sacral/pink; solar plexus/green; heart/gold; throat/blue; third eye/indigo; crown/purple. Once you develop your chakras, you might experience different color patterns within the human energy field.

For now, I ask you accept the metaphor I present for the chakra/color archetypes. Consider these correspondences between the chakras as reference points for learning.

Chakras are archetypes for the energies of creation. Being energy (and aspects of the Universe), each archetype vibrates. The frequency of each varies with the essence of their respective energy. However, an archetype symbolizes more of a gamut of frequencies rather than one specific vibration. For example, in Greek and Roman mythology, the god Mercury archetype exemplifies the highest form of intellect and communication. This "god" was also associated with trickery and deceit.

If you have read *Chakra Mastery*, please bear with me, as I am repeating a metaphor relevant to understanding archetypes, colors and chakras. Modern radio provides a corresponding, although linear, analogy to this seeming paradox of a range of behaviors contained within an archetype.

FM (frequency modulated) radio is received in the RF (radio frequency) spectrum starting at 88 megahertz (88 million of cycles per second) through 108 MHz. This range, or group of frequencies, is referred to as bandwidth. (There are a multitude of bands in the RF spectrum — Ham radio operators are assigned specific bandwidths, cell phones have defined broadcast frequencies, etc. – our airwaves are very busy!)

Various FM radio stations broadcast on a specific frequency within the bandwidth. You dial up a specific frequency in order to "tune" into a station. In a similar manner, you can "tune" into an aspect of the archetype's energy by "dialing" its corresponding frequency in the bandwidth.

Following the assumption that the higher the vibratory rate, the closer to spirit, the stations at the upper end of the FM band correspond to the higher expression of the archetype. The stations at the lower end of the band correlate to the grosser energies associated with the archetype. Concluding this analogy, Mercury as the trickster would be 88.5 MHz on the dial while Mercury as the master would be 107.9 MHz.

The musical scale metaphorically describes this dynamic range of archetypal energy. Esoteric practices often refer to either the higher or the lower octave of an archetypal energy. When we express the higher octave of an archetype, we are referring to a greater, or faster, frequency. A specific tone, when sounded an octave higher, vibrates at twice the rate as the lower note. Higher octaves of a specific tone occur at frequencies to the power of two.

Assume that a certain aspect of your consciousness resonates to a specific vibratory rate. Who you are, how you perceive your world, is determined by this vibratory rate. You have a unique vibratory rate, or pitch, just like a violin string can produce a certain pitch by placing a finger at a specific point along the string.

As an archetype, each chakra corresponds to physical and psychological qualities. Each is associated with nerve ganglia (plexus), endocrine gland(s), organ(s) of the body and an area of the body. As well, each energy center corresponds to one of the six senses —smell, taste, sight, touch, hearing and ESP.

Each chakra carries the essence of specific energy patterns, optimum actions, a life quality and overall quality. On a soul level, each contains a fundamental lesson. In *Chakra Mastery*, I review each chakra and present a grid of the correspondences, including the Sanskrit name and seed sound. A summary of these attributes appears in Chapter 13.

Your soul lesson may be easy or challenging. Possibly it may be at the forefront of your life's experiences. You may not be aware of your soul lesson on a conscious level. Yet it still influences your life in mysterious ways until you choose to embrace the lesson and resolve outstanding issues.

Each chakra's archetypal energy runs a gamut of emotions, experiences and expressions. They are archetypes that provide your energy blueprint for physical incarnation—your energetic template. Each person's chakras are unique—remember, these are archetypes, not absolutes. You have free will to express these energies in your life.

As each color of the seven spectral colors represents a range of frequencies, each chakra archetype also has a corresponding range of expressions. Within this range are lower and upper octave vibrations. The upper, or higher octave vibrates at a faster frequency and represents positive, growth oriented energy patterns. Consider the higher octave as leading to the "Master Path." Lower octave, or slower, frequencies are denser and attract negative, stagnating energy. Resonating with lower octave energies keeps you on the student path.

Which octave of expression do you want to resonate to and how do you get there? All vibrations—both upper and lower octaves— resonate with the great vibration creator, your thoughts. Thoughts beget emotions or

E-motions—energy in motion. You can choose thoughts that are the higher octave expression of a chakra's archetypal energy.

When you awaken to higher vibrations—vibrate differently and resonate to higher frequencies—you need less sleep. Increase of vibration allows your chakras to rotate at a faster rate and therefore process information in real time as events occur. As you evolve, your chakras spin faster and expand their influence within your HES.

How do you get to the higher octave? It's important to strengthen your energy field. Imagine creating a cocoon of strong, clear energy around yourself. Powerful, energetic chakras radiate a cohesive, strong aura. Only those vibrations that are the same as or higher can then penetrate your personal energy field, your aura, so you need to maintain a frequency that resonates with higher vibrations.

What is Color?

*"If you want to find the secrets of the universe,
think in terms of energy, frequency and vibration . . . "* ~Nikola Tesla

CAROLYN WHITE PHD

To fully understand the nature of color and how it relates to us energetically, we must first understand the Universe is defined by the electromagnetic spectrum. The difference between you and a table is your vibrational rate is different from the table's.

What is the electromagnetic spectrum? Basically, it is the frequency range of electromagnetic energy, measured in Hertz (Hz), which is one cycle per second. The fewer cycles per second, the slower the vibration, and the denser the energy. This chart bests illustrates the concept:

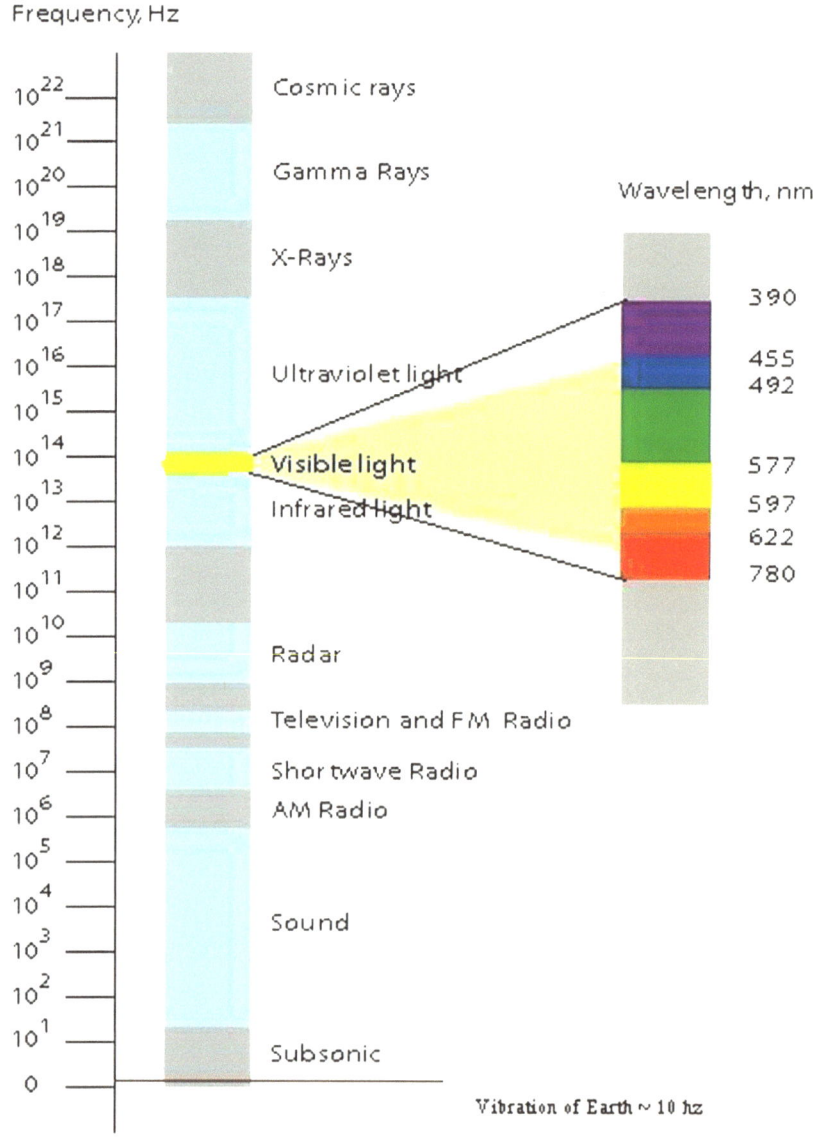

Note sound has a lower frequency, or cycles per second, than visible light. Sound also has a greater range of frequency than visible light.

Humans are wired with five common senses to register specific frequency ranges. With our ears, we can hear sounds vibrating within the range of 60 Hz to around 23,000 Hz. Consider dogs discern sounds from 60 Hz to 45,000 Hz (45 kHz) while Beluga whales' sensitivity starts at 1,000 Hz and peaks at 123,000 Hz. The porpoise has the greatest hearing range of mammals, going from 75 Hz to 150,000 Hz.

Our skin (touch) and tongue (taste) sense infrared light, which we call heat. If we stay out in the sun too long, even on a cloudy day, our skin registers ultra-violet light with burns and blisters.

Many other frequencies vibrate within the Universe—it's just that our human body is not "wired" to directly detect these frequencies. AM radio waves, vibrating at a higher frequency than audible sound, are meaningless unless we use a radio receiver built to tune into these frequencies and "translate" them into an audible range. Cell phones capture frequencies above the television and FM radio range—Ultra High Frequency (UHF). Think about it—millions of waves of electromagnetic energy are buzzing around you at any given time. From phone conversations, TV programs, radio transmissions and satellite signals we live in a sea of vibration and frequency.

Remember I discussed the Hermetic Law of Correspondence and frequencies? I'm often asked how evoking one energetic form can attract another, similar form. The cellular phone operates on these principles of frequency, resonance and harmonics. Depending on where you are in the world, cellular phone transmissions are broadcast between 800 MHz and 1900 MHz of the electromagnetic spectrum. This range is above audible sound.

Yet, when you answer a phone call, you hear the words of the caller. How? Simply, the cellular phone "translates" the vibration and frequency of the UHF into audible sound based on the principle of harmonics.

The human eye is calibrated to be sensitive to a very narrow band within the enormous range of frequencies of the electromagnetic spectrum. This narrow band of frequencies is referred to as the visible light spectrum.

Visible light—that which is detectable by the human eye—consists of wavelengths ranging from approximately 780 nanometer (7.80×10^{-7} m) down to 390 nanometer (3.90×10^{-7} m). Specific wavelengths within the spectrum correspond to a specific color based upon how humans typically perceive light of that wavelength. The long wavelength end of the spectrum corresponds to red light and the short wavelength end of the spectrum corresponds to violet light. Other colors within the spectrum include orange, yellow, green, blue and indigo. The graphic below depicts the approximate range of wavelengths associated with the various perceived colors within the spectrum.

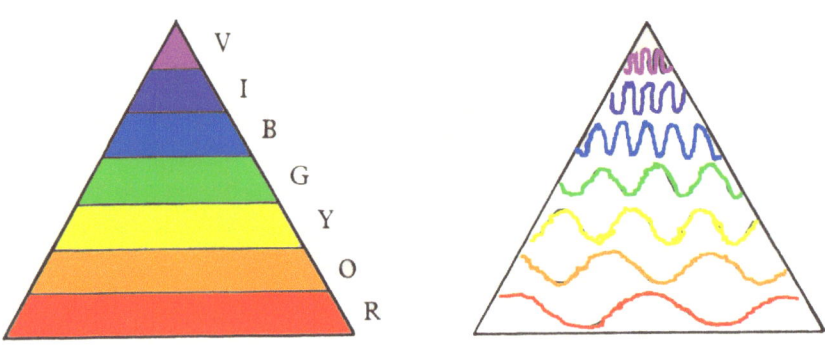

Color is our physiological and psychological response to electromagnetic energy of a specific frequency or a set of frequencies entering our eyes. When the full range within the visible light spectrum enters our eyes, we perceive "white light."

Color Me Healthy Wealthy and Wise

Creating Color

Confusion often arises concerning what's what with color primaries, mixing colors, etc. Essentially, colors fall into one of two categories: Light and Chemistry.

Light—The Additive Principle

When light produces color, it's called the additive principle. All the colors of light along the visible light spectrum combine to create white light. The primary colors of light—those that combine in various degrees to produce secondary colors—are red, green and blue/violet. This phenomenon is due to the color receptors in our eyes, the cones, tuned, or calibrated, to perceive red, green and blue/violet. Perhaps you have seen "RGB" cable connection referenced on your computer or TV. Since computer screens and TV monitors create their output with light, they use the additive principle of creating color for your viewing pleasure.

The additive principle comes into play when using light for color therapy as some of the color wheel properties, such as complementary colors, differ from colors created via chemistry.

PRIMARIES OF **LIGHT**
RED, GREEN, BLUE/VIOLET

Note white light, in the middle, results when the three primaries of light are combined.

Chemistry—The Subtractive Principle

The principle of creating colors through chemistry is referred to as subtractive color. A specific color is produced by combining pigments derived from rocks, minerals, plants and animals subjected to chemical extraction processes. Nature also creates her colors through biological processes.

Why subtractive? When we see a physical color of an object, it is absorbing the entire spectrum of all the light illuminating it except the "color" that it is. A green leaf is absorbing all frequencies of light except the "green" frequency. A red sweater absorbs all frequencies of light except the "red" frequency. The primary colors of pigments—a group of colors from which all other colors can be obtained by mixing—are red, yellow and blue.

Consider that white light consists of the three primary colors of light—red, green and blue. If white light is shining on a shirt, then its primaries—red, green and blue light— are shining on the shirt as well. If the shirt absorbs blue light, then only red and green light will be reflected from the shirt. So while red, green and blue light shine upon the shirt, only red and green light will reflect from it. Red and green light striking your eye always gives the appearance of yellow; for this reason, the shirt will appear yellow.

Technically, light is not really "colored." Light is simply electromagnetic energy with a specific wavelength or a mixture of wavelengths. It has no "color" in and of itself. An object that is emitting or reflecting light to our eyes appears to have a specific color as the result of our eye-brain response to the wavelength.

Consequently, the color of objects is not in the object per se. Rather the color results from the light that reflects off or transmits through the object. The chemical nature of the pigments present in the object enables it to absorb certain frequencies of light. Depending on the frequency range of light hitting the object, the observer will have their subjective experience of the color. Artists who paint refer to this sensation as "local" color. Intellectually, you might view a forest of trees as "green" yet, due to the light hitting this forest, the artist sees the color as blue.

To fully activate the effects of color, you need light. If you walk into a dark room, can your eyes discern the color of the objects? If you rely on your eyes to perceive color, then light enhances your experience with color.

Interestingly, some blind individuals can sense different colors via touch. Are they using their sense of touch to discriminate the frequencies of the visible light spectrum? People blind from birth often have adapted their sense of hearing to navigate life—are they able to "hear" the sound of a specific wave length and relate this to a color?

In the 1970's, Carol Anne Liarso worked with the blind from birth, helping them to "see" color. She taught her clients to concentrate on the brow (third-eye) chakra, which corresponds with the pineal gland. Lairso instructed them to think light, even though they had never seen light or color. Through practice and coaching, one individual was able to discern light waves of energy around objects via the brow center. This woman demonstrated her learned ability to discriminate shapes by their light wave signature.

PRIMARIES OF **PIGMENTS** —
CHEMISTRY.
RED, YELLOW, BLUE

Note black is formed when the three primary pigments are combined. Black is not a color, as it is technically colorless from the complete absorption of light.

Why is all this information about color, light, chemistry and sensation important? Remember, light is energy vibrating at varying frequencies.

Color is a sensation of this light, which, if you want to elicit a specific archetypal energy, you can call on this energy via the color. What color and how you use it is important.

When working with the aura and chakras, to tonify, or strengthen, I recommend using the predominate aura color. If you need to energize any of the seven major chakras, use the archetypal color representing each one. If you want to attract a specific energy vibration into your life or a situation, use the color associated with that archetype.

If you need to balance an area of your life—i.e. you are over-anxious (root chakra/red)— then use the complementary color for that chakra or archetypal energy. A complementary color is the color opposite on the color wheel.

Here's where the information about additive and subtractive colors enters the picture: The complementary colors for Light (additive) are slightly different from pigmented (subtractive) objects.

If you are using a light source, translucent gemstone or a crystal to balance a specific energy, then you look at the color wheel for the light spectrum—the seven spectral colors. Consider anything that is translucent, as a window shade that lets a high degree of light through, as a candidate for using the light spectrum.

If you are using a pigmented object, clothing, décor, or an opaque gemstone, then you look at the color wheel for pigmented colors. Most artists color wheels represent the subtractive system. Think in terms of solid, i.e. light cannot easily shine through.

The Seven Spectral Colors Wheel represents the spectral colors for light. The complementary colors for each spectral color are:

Blue — Red

Indigo — Orange

Yellow — Violet

Green — Magenta

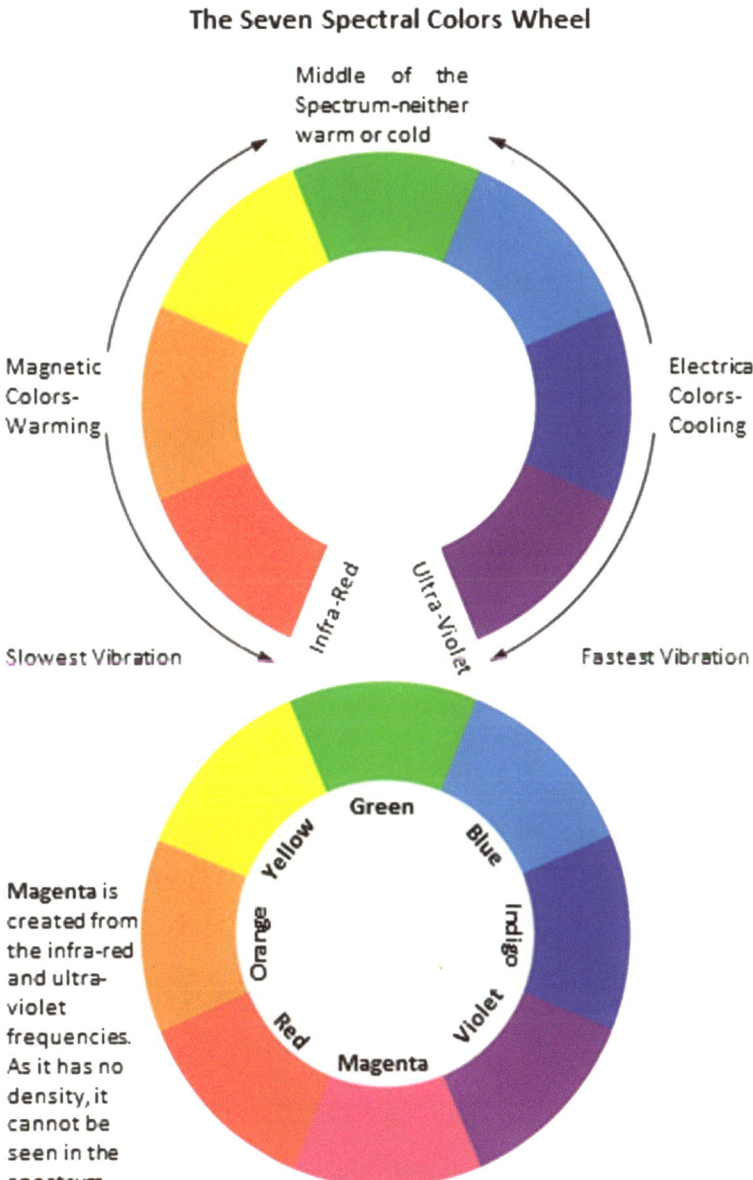

Several modalities that use the properties of light are:

- Light Therapy using colored light filters
- Drinking Solarized Water filtered through colored glass
- Transparent/translucent Crystal Therapy
- Sunlight exposure

Sunlight has all the aspects of the rainbow colors. We require all 7 primary colors of the light spectrum to maintain good mental, emotional and physical health. Light affects all aspects of our biochemical system. The premise is light is a living being—the original energy of creation. Let there be light and there will be life. Sunlight entrains to subtle, etheric bodies of aura.

Exposure to the sun's rays has garnered considerable controversy in 21st century medicine. Allopathic medicine believes it is the sole cause of melanoma, skin cancers. A more holistic health approach suggests there are many other factors to this dis-ease, including diet, exposure to toxins and even the sun blocks used on the skin.

Dr. Ott, renowned for his research on eye health and light, recommends regular exposure to sunlight without usage of sunglasses.

My younger son, born in 1982, experienced a bit of jaundice several days after his birth due to elevated levels of bilirubin. At that time, my doctor, who was also a mother, prescribed exposing his naked body to sunlight a couple of times per day—once in the morning and once in the afternoon. After several days, the jaundice disappeared and his bilirubin levels were normal.

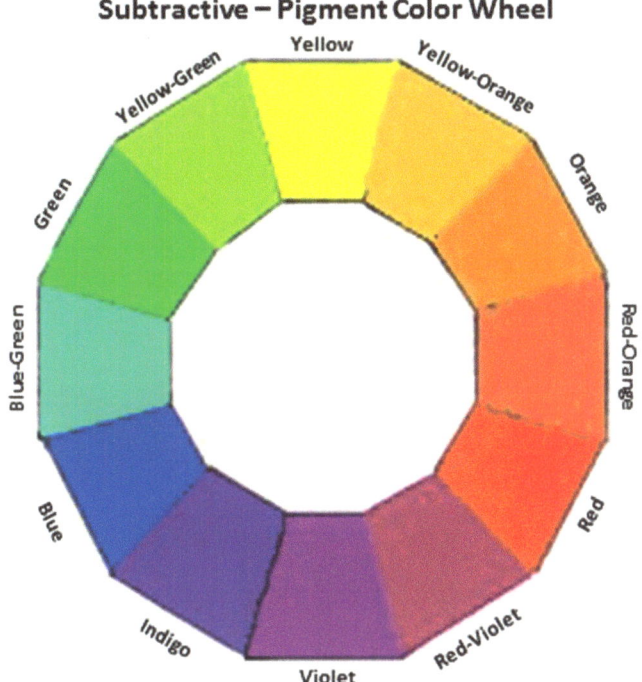

In some respects, it's easier to work with the subtractive properties of color as you can incorporate various objects, décor or clothing into your environment. Additionally, several nuances are readily available to fine tune the desired effect via color properties.

The complementary subtractive colors are:

Yellow —Violet (Same as additive complementary)

Blue—Orange

Red—Green

Color Properties

When working with colors in clothing, objects or décor, certain color characteristics provide different stimulus functions. These color characteristics – tint, shade, tone – are aspects or properties of each color. Looking at a subtractive color wheel helps in visualizing these characteristics.

Hue —this is the pure color. Use for activating and deeply focusing your energy. Hues connect with the core archetypes of the color.

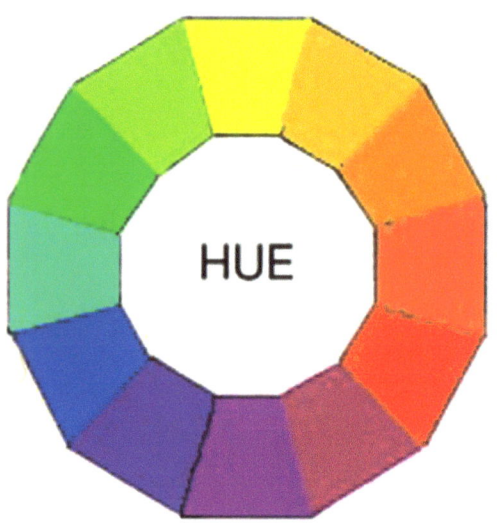

Tint — A Hue, or color, with white added. Tints are stimulating, uplifting, and bright. Tints are pastels.

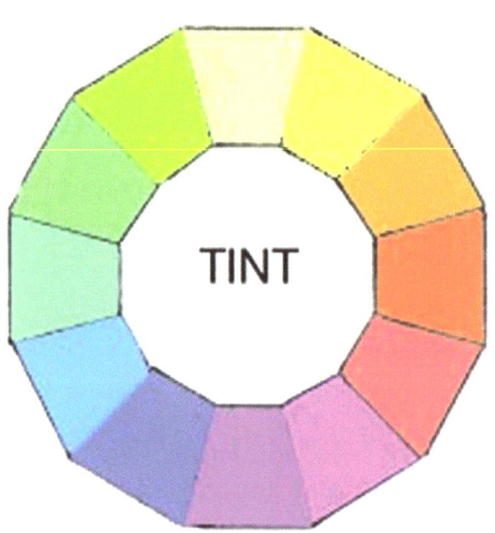

COLOR ME HEALTHY WEALTHY AND WISE

Tone — A color with gray added. Tones are calming, relaxing and muted.

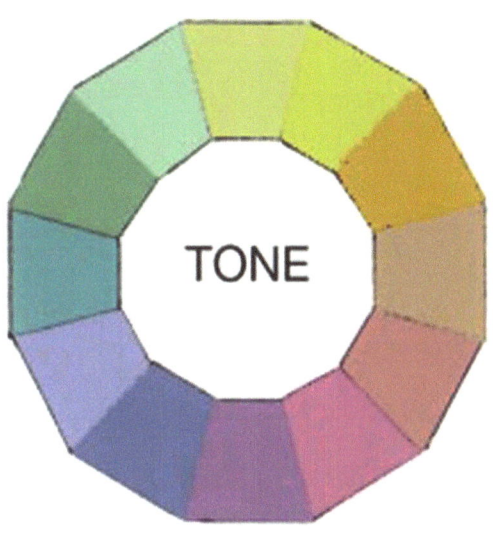

Shade — A color with black pigment added. Shades are centering, dynamic and intense.

When working with a challenging area of life, you may want to use either a tone or shade, as the color is more subtle. Many do not like orange, so you might want to incorporate a tone or shade of orange to bring that color into your vibrational field.

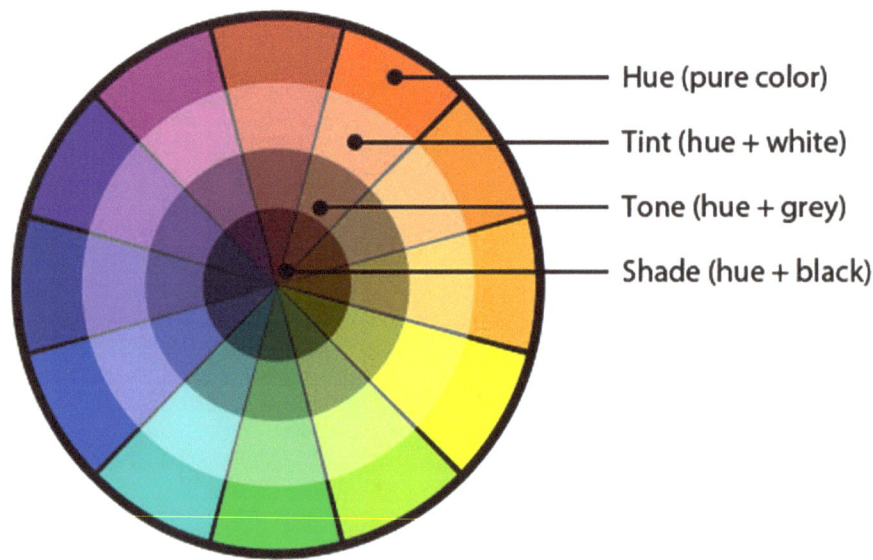

Working with Color

"Colors are vibrating light energies, each 'color ray' produces a sound that affects matter."

~Jacqueline Ripstein

Working with Color—Key Concepts

Colors have properties responding to our sensations. Additionally, certain colors correspond to specific aspects of our physical body.

Colors of a slower vibratory rate are considered warm, magnetic colors. Look at the Electromagnetic spectrum scale at the beginning of Chapter 2. Red, yellow and orange are warm colors. Note that red is slightly higher in frequency than infra-red, which is heat. Yellow and orange are usually associated with the warmth of the sun.

Green is considered a neutral color, being in the middle of the visible light spectrum. Green can have both warm properties, as in yellow-green, to cool, as in blue-green. Magenta, a mixture of infra-red and ultra-violet from the light spectrum, is neutral.

Blue, indigo and violet are cool, electric colors. Violet is a slightly lower frequency than ultra-violet.

Traditionally, the following systems of the body are assigned to a color family:

Muscular — Red

Circulatory — Orange

Nervous — Yellow

Digestive — Green

Respiratory — Blue

Skeletal — Indigo

Violet, associated with the crown chakra, is not considered in this equation as the crown chakra is not connected with the spine and central nervous system.

All acute dis-eases are "hot" dis-eases and are usually associated with a fever, i.e. influenza.

All chronic dis-eases are conditions without a fever and considered "cool" conditions, i.e. arthritis.

All "hot" dis-eases are corrected or balanced with cool colors.

All "cool" dis-eases are balanced with warm colors.

If you are in doubt as to the coolness or warmness of a physical condition, start with green.

From an energetic perspective, red and green have a greater impact on the physical level. If you experience a fever from an infection caused by a cut, then green is the most effective. Chronic pain from a sports injury would probably respond to red and heat.

Conditions that are emotional in nature, such as an injury from an accident or an acute condition with an emotional charge respond best to orange or blue. If you believe a mental condition exists surrounding the dis-ease, then yellow works best. Violet, especially the violet flame, helps when a dis-ease has a spiritual component.

Notes:

How to Work with Color Everyday

"If I can put one touch of rosy sunset into the life of any man or woman, I shall feel that I have worked with God." ~ G.K. Chesterton

Since we all live in our mind and thoughts, color is a powerful ally in shaping your thoughts. Each color has a higher vibration and lower vibrational energy, which can impact your mental attitude. Combined with your mind, color, when used appropriately, has a very life-affirming effect on your body and spirit.

Consider the tints of hues are more uplifting and, since a tint contains white, are more spiritual. Use tints when you want to quiet your mind and view life from a more spiritual, rather than a physical, standpoint.

Pure hues are dynamic and bring the greatest energy to bear. In some circumstances, discretions and subtleness are the best strategy. Tones and shades provide just that ingredient of color without being overbearing. Consider tones as having more yin, or passive qualities with shades being more yang, or active.

If you are dealing with an argumentative person, imagine that person enveloped in a gentle blue tint. Not only will this help you to remain calm, it may even diffuse their anger (red).

Perhaps you got out of bed on the wrong side and are feeling "blue." Imagine you are viewing the world through "rose-colored" glasses. You can transform the energy of your life from negative to positive just by using colors, both in physical reality as well as in your mind. Remember, color is light, which holds and transmits powerful life-affirming energy if you tap into the higher octave vibrations.

Choose to wear a certain color to meet the needs of the day. This is a way of connecting with and sharing a color with others. What vibe do you want to radiate today? Surround yourself with the energy you want to project. Need to communicate? Wear blue. Feel like you need to radiate energy to get things done? Wear red. Want to ramp up your creativity? Bring some orange into your life. Pick an energy signature for your day and wear a color resonating with that energy.

Mentally imagine a helpful color around another person. Consider this as "sending" a color prayer to another person, animal, place or situation. Immerse your prayer focus with that color.

Observe and connect with colors in Nature. Do you watch sunrises and sunset? What colors do you see? Do you notice the colors of birds and animals? During the day, do you notice the brilliant hues of flowers? Do you pay attention to the color of other's clothing? Notice the color of their eyes and complexion? Become aware of the colors.

Take one color per week and make it your own. For example, Orange is the color of joy. Look for it at home, work, in magazine ads, stores, TV programs and in nature. During the week, wear something orange (hint: remember, there are other "oranges" besides pumpkin orange. Select a tint, tone or shade of orange.) Notice how you feel when you spot your color of the week as well as when you wear this color.

Consider which color will help you attain your goals today. What do you want to achieve today? Do you have a health challenge? Dress your body with colors that will improve your health.

Meditate and observe if/what colors appear to you. Mentally note the color(s) and look up their meaning.

Breathe color—take deep, belly breaths as explained in *Chakra Mastery*. When you inhale, imagine you are breathing in a color. Hold your breath and, as you exhale, pay attention and observe if that color has changed. Using greens or blues help calm and center you. Pinks and salmons also bring peace and as warmer colors, promote more activity. Breathing pink assists in forgiving yourself and others. Indigo and violet are spiritually uplifting.

Recently as of this writing, I was involved in a car accident. My significant injuries involved bruising due to my seatbelt. I decided to forego the Western medical treatment of administrating pain "killers" as I wanted my body to respond and heal itself. Yes, I was in pain. To counter this feeling and energize my body to heal, I imagined the color green—a cool aqua green—entering my body with each deep "belly breath." Imagining this healing cool green color did help me ease the pain and assisted my journey to healing naturally.

Many times, I've been asked this question about color breathing: "What happens if I imaging a specific color focused on an area of my body and I just don't 'see' this color or it changes to something else?" If you have the intention of invoking a specific color, yet can't "see" it that is OK. Depending on how you are wired, you might not be a visualizer.

Remember, just having the intention of attracting a color energetically works. If the color you are evoking changes, that's OK too. I tell individuals to enjoy the experience and not get hung up on following exacting standards.

One of my clients lamented he was always trying to envision blue entering his throat area. Every time, the blue change to white. I reminded him to be unattached to outcomes and white, as light, did contain all the spectral colors of the rainbow. Basically, start out with a "color" intention and then "see" what happens. As long as your intention is to work for your highest good, then you are on the right path.

Think color—if you are faced with a challenge or stressful situation, think and project a color which improves your mental and emotional outlook. Ask your body what it needs at the moment. Generally:

- **Reds** stimulate and give the impetus to change and bolster courage. It is the power of action and energy to move you physically and give life. Red is contraindicated if anger is present or an over-stimulated sexual libido. Monitor any usage above the heart or around head.

- **Oranges** bring joy, wisdom and strengthen your will. Also great for digestion. It lends courage and creative expansion.

- **Yellows** are very cleansing and encourage enlightenment leading to illumination. It is the color of consciousness and the logical mind. Great for studying and for feeling good about yourself.

- **Greens** energize and stimulate growth and openness to change. This is the middle of the spectrum. Balancing, harmonizing and healing. Apple green is great for an over-active mind.

- **Blues** give overall calmness, peace and ego control. It is the gateway to relationship with spirit.

- **Indigo** connects with energies from the cosmos, the Universal Energy Field.

- **Violets** bring spiritual balance, harmony and peace. It transmutes and dissolves non-life promoting and stagnant energies. Avoid wearing violet if you are depressed. Choose peach or an orange tint instead to uplift your spirits.

Several other colors you might use in your daily awareness of color:

- **Magenta** is considered the higher octave of red. It's needed in your aura for good organization and administrative tasks. It promotes the spiritual energy of love.

- **Pink** is a tint of red and is softer, more caring than red. Eases irritability and worrying thoughts. A peacemaker color for dealing with family quarrels or difficult people.

- **Turquoise** combines the healing and balancing properties of green and blue, hence it links the heart and throat chakras. Because of this connection, turquoise helps express your words in public speaking. It raises your overall vibrational field.

- **Peach** brings out joy and harmony. It stimulates creativity.

- **Salmon** radiates a universal love for humanity. Often considered the color of unconditional love as it doesn't entrain within the aura until you are a "clear" prism for the light of life.

- **Brown** helps if you want to go within and ground yourself. Linked to security patterns, if worn too extensively, can restrict your energy.

- **Gray** (not silver gray) is half white, half black. It is linked to fear, denying aspects of your true self. If you lack judgment, wear gray.

- **Silver** is a galactic frequency connecting you with inner dimensions.

- **Gold** creates the body of the material world, i.e. manifesting. The alchemists' philosopher's gold was the ultimate tool of manifestation.

- **White** is the combination of all colors of the visible spectrum. It represents fusion on the highest octaves of spiritual energy.

Remember, **Black** is not a color as, in the world of chemical, or subtractive, color properties, it absorbs all colors. Black is the absence of light and therefore, contraindicated for any life-promoting energy work.

Black is so pervasive in our world today, especially in the West. From clothing to phones, the world is painted black. Henry Ford, when advertising his early cars, said, "You can have any color as long as it's black."

By contrast, many Oriental cultures are awash in color, both in their attire and housing. Catholic priests and nuns wear black. Buddhist monks drape themselves in saffron-orange robes. Indian women radiate in flowing colorful saris while every Western woman needs that little black dress.

From my art teachers to several spiritual mentors, I've been admonished about the deleterious impact of black. From the art teacher's perspective, black is to be avoided in classic painting as, being a non-color, it doesn't occur in nature. Observe coal and obsidian—you might think of these as black yet, upon closer examination, coal is dark gray and obsidian, as a volcanic glass, reflects light.

Several of my spiritual mentors have cautioned that wearing black shows the need to step back from the world to feel strong. Most people who wear black feel insecure inside, often wanting to feel anonymous. Perhaps the prevalence of black clothing in Western society shows a general angst and fear of connecting, collectively, with our authentic nature.

Because black used in clothing absorbs all colors, another teacher suggested primarily wearing this color could prematurely wrinkle the skin. Black garments are associated with the black, "negative" energies of witches and vampires. Remember, black is the absence of light. Light is life—the life force energy. You have a choice to live in the light.

Consider black, as an absorber of all the light hitting it, does not "give back" any vibrational frequency. Hence, it has no movement or radiant energy. Black can be used in moderation paired with other colors as it emphasizes the other color, potentially giving "power" to the non-black color. Combined with pink, it lends social power. Red and black evoke physical power and yellow plus black is an intellectual combination.

Next time you wear a black outfit, pay attention to your energy. What do you notice about how your day went, how people interacted with you? Next day, be colorful. Wear your favorite color. Notice how this works for you. Any difference in the energies?

Colors for Children

"The purest and most thoughtful minds are those which love color the most." ~ John Ruskin

Children are very interested in the deeper meanings of color. Their unpolluted minds are curious about their environment and are very aware of energies surrounding them. Be sure to explain to them, as they will be quick to respond to the nuances of their environment.

With so many pressures on children today, getting back to basics with color may help alleviate many physical and mental health issues of today's children.

Ask your child what their favorite color is. We often, as a society, impose prejudices on color and the sex of a child. You may assume pink for a girl and blue for a boy. Yet, I've encountered many young ladies who have an aversion to pink and young lads who love pink.

Generally, children up to the age of sexual maturity are best served by tints of colors. Their chakras and auras are not fully actualized until the late teens to early twenties. Babies who wear bright, full hues and tones or shades of colors often cannot process the energy of these color properties. Unless you keep their surrounding colors as tints, the baby may react, exhibiting aggressive, over-active and restless behavior. Perhaps a contributing factor of attention–deficit disorder lies partially in lack of sensitivity to our children's response to color.

Often, you may have to balance preferential colors with their complementary colors. A child, who predominately loves blue, needs to be surrounded with warm colors, such as peach, to ground their energy.

A child fixated with blue may be too passive and live in their world. One mom responded to her young son wanting his room painted all blue. He was so over-active that it made him feel depressed (blue). When mom introduced the color peach into his room, her son's energy channeled into more creative endeavors. The blue, when balanced with the peach (complementary colors on the subtractive color wheel), still had a calming effect without being depressive.

If your child is drawn to violet, they are very creative and love beauty. They are here on Earth for a special reason. You can help them ground their life's purpose by introducing yellow into their environment (complementary to violet). Peaches and pinks—tints of orange and red—plus soft greens help in creating a soothing and enriched environment.

Colors for a child's bedroom are important as colors have a strong impact on their aura. Remember pastel colors (tints) are best. Choose tints from the warm and cool part of the spectrum to balance energy (complementary colors.)

All children respond to apple green. Apple green and pink together are beautiful and help some of the most difficult behavior issues in children. A quiet child responds to sunshine yellow with soft green and pink/orange in their bedroom.

Yellow tends to bring a child out of themselves. Pink/orange gives a sense of warmth and security. Green brings balance. Children who do not sleep well may respond to a pink light, which is soothing and relaxing. A yellow light is great for a child who lacks concentration at school as well as doing homework.

Orange is being used more today for children, as it has red and yellow in it. This color radiates love and wisdom, brings joy, is uplifting and strengthens the etheric aura.

Orange helps autistic children. A day care center in London, UK, introduced orange cushions into their décor and found a greater response from their autistic children. Painting the walls a tint of orange or peach makes reception areas of pediatrician's offices feel warmer and secure.

Remember to observe the baby/child in their environment and respond to their energy. When you are selecting colors for your child, start with tints and pastels. Keep the color scheme balanced—if the walls are light blue, include some peach or apple green highlights. Introducing the complementary pigment color is effective for bringing about harmony. Too many colors can lead to conflicting energies. As a child develops, vary their exposure to color energies as this is part of their learning process, albeit on a subliminal level.

Notes:

Changing the Energy Within

"Color is the melody of light." ~ Joyce Wycott

I am a great advocate of belly breathing. My book, *Chakra Mastery* details the methods of belly breathing, a way to fill your lungs with life-supporting oxygen. Learning the Master's breath is the most energizing thing you can do for yourself.

Any color you breathe in and hold becomes an actuality. Your cells pick up the energy and the effect becomes more powerful.

You may choose colors specific to your current condition(s). Refer to the tables in Chapter 14 and determine which color will assist a specific condition. For example, if you have a headache, breathing in green can ease the pain. As you inhale with a "belly breath," imagine a soft green entering through your heart area and then enveloping your head. Hold, then exhale, paying attention to any colors you experience while exhaling breath.

A soft green is recommended as a starting point for any pain issues. Breathing either green or a cool blue and directing it into the abdominal area helps relieve women's menstrual cramps. A cool green, blue- green or blue helps any pain with a hot, stabling sensation.

Can't sleep at night? Gently and slowly breathe in a soft pink or salmon, filling your lungs and then slowly exhale. Just as a pink light in a child's bedroom can help them sleep, using pink or salmon balances out your bloodstream and brings peace to your night's rest.

Breathing color is a powerful ally when you combine with affirmations appropriate to the color. To reinforce the effect, repeat the affirmation seven times. Close your eye and imaging the color pouring into your being.

Color breathing combined with affirmations is a great self-help method of changing the energy within. These color breathing affirmations are best done in the morning to charge your energy, as before bed may over-energize you.

In your daily practice, you may breathe through and affirm each color. You might affirm one color per day. It really depends on your intent. Note the pure hue of red is not included in the color affirmations as it's generally too strong and is contraindicated for any heart issues.

If you are proficient with visualizations, imagine you are inhaling the warm colors—red, orange and yellow—from Mother Earth through the soles of your feet. Visualize green as entering your body from the surrounding area through your diaphragm/lower chest. Imagine the cool colors—blue, indigo and violet—as coming from the Universal Energy Field, entering your body through the top of your head.

You may start your color breathing by imagining white light entering your body via the top of your head. Imagine this light of life enveloping your body. Envision you are immersed in the light for a minute or two. Affirm this white light is for your highest good. Remember, white light is the expression of all the spectral colors and holds all their properties. If you are unsure of a color to affirm or begin with, ask the white light for direction.

The following page offers a list of color affirmations. Use these with color breathing or as a daily chakra/energy balancing meditation.

Color Affirmations

Pink—Pink is pouring into me, cleansing and purifying the bloodstream, giving me strength and energy for this day. I inhale through the soles of my feet, bringing pink up to the solar plexus and flooding my whole body with its energy.

Rose—Rose is pouring into my blood stream, giving me new life and courage for all I have to do.

Orange—Orange is giving me vitality, Joy, recharging me and my etheric field and balancing my immune system. Orange rejuvenates every part of me.

Yellow—Yellow feeds and nourishes my body, mind and soul. Yellow connects me with wisdom.

Green— Green flows through my heart. Green balances me and brings peace and harmony into my life and all my affairs. It is so.

Turquoise—Turquoise brings peace and calms my mind and emotions.

Blue—Blue brings healing to every cell, tissue and part of my Being. My mind is calm and I am surrounded by a heavenly blue for peace and my highest good.

Indigo—Indigo links me with Higher Knowledge and understanding that will help me at this time. It heals my etheric body.

Violet—Violet cleanses and clears the glands and endocrine system within me. Violet purifies me and spiritually connects me with the highest and noblest truths.

Magenta—Magenta heals my body, mind and emotions. It brings me a deeper understanding of all my affairs, going forward knowing all is well.

Color, Light and Interior States

Color breathing and affirmations will have a demonstrable impact on improving your inner and outer being. Color can also have a positive impact on the general populace.

As detailed in the list of color properties in Chapter 14, blue has a calming and relaxing effect, bringing harmony and balance. LED blue streetlights installed in several Tokyo urban areas have prevented suicides and street crime. This finding encouraged a number of Japanese railway companies to install blue-light-emitting apparatus at stations to prevent people from committing suicide by jumping in front of trains.

Anti-suicide barriers around the tracks don't deter the jumper with intent to end their life. Statistics compiled by JR East, one of Japan's largest train companies, indicate suicides occurring at its stations rose from 42 in 2006 to 58 in 2007 and 68 in 2008. Since Japan relies on its light-rail transit system to move thousands of people daily, a suicide, besides being a human tragedy, brings the system to a halt.

Railway companies that have already installed the blue lighting say they have played a successful role in preventing suicides. Keihin Electric Express Railway Co. changed the color of eight lights on the ends of platforms at Gumyoji Station in Yokohama, Japan, in February 2008. According to the company, every year several people attempt to commit suicide at this station. No suicide attempts have occurred at the station since the blue lighting was introduced. The blue lighting seems to calm the psyche of a would-be jumper.

Blue lighting seems to deter criminal activity as well. In 2005, the Nara, Japan, prefecture police installed blue street lights in their district. Subsequently, crimes decreased by about 9 percent in blue-illuminated neighborhoods.

In 2000, Glasgow, Scotland, introduced blue street lighting to improve the city's night-time landscape. Afterward, the number of crimes in areas illuminated in blue noticeably decreased.

Blue illumination is used for other purposes than preventing crimes and suicides. In 2001, 152 blue lights were installed along a 1.8-kilometer stretch of the Tomei Expressway near the Tokyo interchange to prevent accidents.

A spokesman of Central Nippon Expressway Co. commented, "The illumination was introduced as part of our efforts to encourage people to drive safely by instinctively and emotionally appealing to them to calm down."[1]

According to Professor Tsuneo Suzuki at Keio University in Japan, "There are a number of pieces of data to prove blue has a calming effect upon people. However, it's an unusual color for lighting, so people may just feel like avoiding standing out by committing crimes or suicide under such unusual illumination. It's a little risky to believe that the color of lighting can prevent anything."[2]

I agree with the professor that blue does have a very calming influence on people. I believe Professor Suzuki is missing the point when he opines the color of lighting is not a preventative. Light is a living being, with specific frequencies carrying a message. When this vibrational "message" permeates an area, most life-forms will entrain with the frequency. Consequently, a natural shift occurs in the mind-set of those exposed to this frequency.

An agitated mind, entering into the sphere of blue light's influence, would tend to calm. Blue cools any angry, impulsive emotions and actions. Would the individual contemplating suicide or a robbery still go through with their deed? Perhaps— and not in the areas flooded with blue light, as this calming influence doesn't lend itself to the stage of their life's drama.

Other colors of light assist in altering internal states. Children and adults who do not sleep well may respond to a pink light in their bedroom, which is soothing and relaxing. A yellow light helps with concentration and studying.

Even interior "white" lights can impact your mood and energy. Fluorescent lights—even full-spectrum ones—create electromagnetic (EM) noise. These EM frequencies not only wreak havoc with sensitive instruments, they can cause headache, eye strain and feelings of anxiety and irritation.

I noticed this effect on our sailboat, which was equipped with both a long-range SSB radio and short-range VHF radio. When we had regular fluorescent tube lighting, every time we fired up either radio, we'd hear a crackling, static noise. We eliminated this problem at first by turning off the lights. Eventually, we upgraded to shielded, EM filtered fluorescent lights at a cost four times of a "normal" tube light.

If you ever feel uneasy in a large interior shopping center, perhaps it's your reaction to EM noise from the lighting. Many facilities can't afford to equip these lights with the shielding and filters to remove this noise.

LED white lights for interior usage didn't catch on until the light was transformed from a cold, bluish-purple cast to a warm yellow light. Unlike the totally blue lights installed in Scotland and Japan, the cold white LED's imparted a hard-to-see feeling, which seemed too harsh. Warmer colors in the LED white give a softer appearance for all areas illuminated.

Besides emitting negative ions when lit, Himalayan salt lamps radiate a warm orange glowing light in the surrounding area. Ambient orange and yellow-orange lights, like candle light, impart a comfortable and emotionally satisfying energy. Luther Burbank discovered plants grow faster and healthier when exposed to orange light.

Pay attention to the lighting in your environment. If you experience discomfort in a certain area of your home, turn the lights off. Do you start to "feel" better? What happens if you introduce non-fluorescent full-spectrum lighting? Natural sunlight is the best source of light, as the "white" light contains all the spectral colors.

Notes:

---

[1]http://inventorspot.com/articles/japan_fights_train_station_suicide_blue_led_lighting_32608#sthash.Z0rJZDDs.dpuf

[2]http://www.seattletimes.com/nation-world/blue-streetlights-believed-to-prevent-

CRYSTAL MAGIC

"Crystals are a living energy...Mother Earth's gifts to us, formed within Her body. In a mystical and beauty-full way, they are the keys to the Universe." ~Angie Karan

Crystals are magic from the core of Mother Earth, grown over years. Fashioned within the Earth, crystals affect the area where they grow. Their presence energizes Mother Earth.

What are crystals? Crystal is the Greek word for ice, *krystallis*. A crystal is a mineral's expression of its invisible, internal atomic structure. Each mineral is naturally composed of elements, such as oxygen, found in our Universe.

Since each mineral grows its own unique geometric shape, the form helps to identify the mineral. Crystals grow in six basic systems or shapes— isometric (cubic), hexagonal, tetragonal, orthorhombic, monoclinic and triclinic.

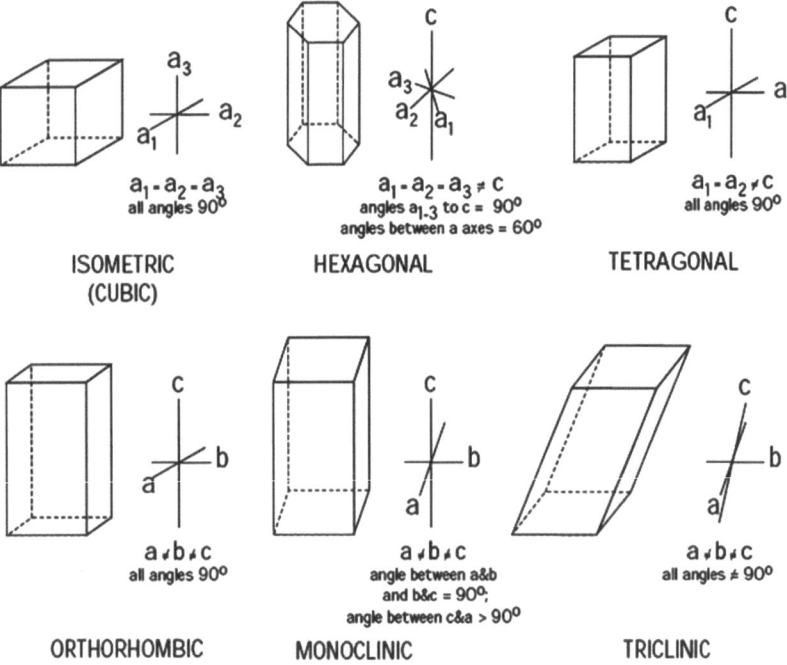

Gemstones are minerals of outstanding clarity, transparency, color purity and perfection. A mineral, in crystal form, may be faceted such as a diamond cut. The mineral may be carved and polished into a cabochon like a turquoise stone mounted in a ring.

Often, you might hear the word "stone" and "rock" in reference to crystal work. Technically, a "rock" is an aggregate of several minerals, formed by one of three processes—igneous, sedimentary and metamorphic. Igneous rocks originate from the hot, fiery, magma from Earth's core. Sedimentary rocks result from the transformation of existing rocks by wind, water, weather and living organisms. Metamorphic rocks are produced by chemical and physical forces, such as an earthquake, that permanently alter the original rock's form.

Crystals can grow in any rock, even on a particle of dust, when a sufficient mineral-rich solution is present. Not all minerals are in crystal form, which makes crystals special.

Elementals, which are nature spirits, oversee the mineral kingdom and can only evolve with our help. Crystals are Mother Earth's gift to create perfect harmonious balance within the Earth and her passengers. Essentially, crystals:

- Maintain energy field of Earth and Solar system.
- Maintain the balance of all electromagnetic fields surrounding Earth
- Balance magnetic energy flow between North and South Poles
- Balance electromagnetic energy moving around the planet with magnetic flow of energy

If you were to view this pattern of energies from above the Earth, it would appear like a web, composed of a flowing grid-like, interconnected energy field.

As I detailed in the Human Energy System (HES) section of *Chakra Mastery,* this same electromagnetic field exists around everything. You have a similar energy field around your body, represented by your aura.

The human body is like a liquid crystal. Each cell and organ has its own balanced electromagnetic field. All are interconnected and interact. When the cell's or organ's field becomes "unbalanced"—the "force" is disturbed—dis-ease manifests. When the balance is restored, healing begins and homeostasis is restored. Essentially, this is the principle of working with crystals to heal, clear and balance the chakras—our HES.

While all crystals have beneficial gifts, those composed of the element silicon have the greatest capacity for working with our HES. Silicon combines with the element oxygen, to form the most common mineral on the Earth's continents, quartz. Quartz is found in most of the Earth's sand—in sandstone, in the world's deserts, riverbeds and beaches. Quartz is the most common mineral composing the granites and gneiss found in Earth's deep continental crusts.

Quartz is two parts oxygen one part silicon —$SiO2$—commonly called silica. As silica is the major mineral in natural quartz, it is also the major mineral in the human body. Silica is abundant on Earth as well as in the human brain. The brain, spinal cord and nerve fibers all need large amounts of silica. From silica we maintain our nails, hair, and our skin sheen, resilience and smoothness. This mineral promotes healthy bone growth and, in a plant-sourced supplement, supports bone growth better than calcium supplements. [1]

Essentially, silica serves the same purpose as crystals for our body as it helps maintain energy fields within and around the body. As it conducts and stores energy, silica gives a piezoelectric quality to our body as it receives and transmits energy.

The Chakra Gemstone Correspondences Guide in Chapter 15, pages 126-127, is annotated with the stone's primary mineral composition. If you are building a gemstone energy kit, I recommend gathering stones containing quartz and silicates first. You will probably see more immediate results with either due to their effectiveness in processing energy.

---

[1] http://www.mercola.com/nutritionplan/advanced_supplements.htm

How do Crystals Energetically Assist You?

Besides the therapeutic color value of each stone, each crystal or gemstone has a physical basis for its energetic properties. Most of the stones associated with each chakra include varieties of quartz, the most abundant mineral in Creation. Interestingly, the name "quartz" is derived from a German word meaning "ancient times." So, quartz connects us with the Ancient and Inner wisdom of cultures long past that had a great appreciation and reverence for our Mother Earth. As quartz is the most common mineral on Earth, it reminds us that this knowledge is available to all—you can resonate with this abundance if you choose to do so.

Quartz exhibits remarkable properties in receiving, sending, and storing electromagnetic energy. Quartz plates "keep time" in modern watches. In the computing industry, all silicon semiconductors are made from quartz—just think of the information that seems to be instantaneously transferred and stored inside your computer! Before the transistor, quartz "crystals" controlled frequencies in all radios.

If you have a specific intention for attracting energy, a variety of quartz assists you in "tuning in" the desired frequency, or energetic vibration. This is due to the precise geometric pattern which forms a crystal's molecular structure. This geometric pattern creates a base resonant frequency producing a precise energetic pattern. By evoking this vibration, eventually, though entrainment, you will resonate with the vibratory energy.

This entrainment occurs as your body also contains and uses silica. Your brain, spinal cord, and nerve fibers all require large amounts of silica to efficiently communicate messages throughout the body. Eating oats, green veggies, carrots, red berries, egg yolks, figs, and nuts replenishes your body's requirements for silica.

Over the years, I've found individuals with healthy plant-based eating habits respond more readily to crystals in their energy field. Perhaps this is due to the levels of silica in their bodies. If you do take silica supplements, ensure they are plant-based, such as horsetails or bamboo, and come from an organic source. Silica is a vital healing component in

Bentonite clay, which can be used on the skin as well as taken internally for cleansing.[2] Check with your health care practitioner if you question the levels of silica in your body.

---

[2] http://www.naturalnews.com/030830_silica_bentonite_clay.html

Crystals and Gemstone Shapes

"A turquoise given by a loving hand carries with it happiness and good fortune." ~ Arabic proverb

Crystals and Gemstones Shapes and Energy Work

When working with energy, sometimes it is best to set your intentions and then "let go and let God/Source/Spirit" take over. When you place quartz gemstones in your energy field, i.e. on your physical body, you are attracting the desired vibration without having to consciously think about your intention.

Certain shapes of crystals or minerals serve different purposes following their form. Like any tool, function follows the form a mineral takes. The following describes potential usages for energy work using various forms of crystals and minerals.

Clusters—Energy Collectors and Disbursers

Amethyst Cluster

Crystal clusters are concentrated and powerful. Think of clusters as hundreds of tiny antennae collectively gathering energy from the Universe and scattering it throughout the surrounding area. If you could see the energetic impact, it would look like a soft, gentle snowfall of fairy dust around its space.

Programming a cluster with love attracts higher vibrational energy to the area. Wear a cluster over your heart to enhance your energy by 200%.

As detailed in chapter 10, amethyst clusters are excellent for cleansing other crystals. Amethyst clusters act as energetic air purifiers, which is why they are excellent for home and office décor. Clusters are energetic air fresheners.

Crystal clusters are often found in geodes—a roundish cavity in a sedimentary rock lined with crystals. When hunting or purchasing "break-at-home" geodes and you have two of the same size, the lighter one will yield more crystals.

Points—Energy Directors

Quartz with single terminated points

Crystals terminated with points at one or both ends direct energy to a specific area. Points emit, transmit or draw out energy, depending on your intentions.

Quartz and its family of crystals—amethyst, citrine, aventurine, rose and smoky quartz—form these classic hexagonal, often prismatic crystals frequently terminated by double hexagonal pyramids. Essentially, these crystals have six facets, or faces, at one or both ends, and terminate into a point.

When searching for a quartz crystal destined for focused work, ensure it has six facets on one end and a clean point. The facet sizes may vary. Think of the six faces corresponding to the six major chakras and the point is the crown.

Every naturally occurring crystal is unique in its creation and all quartz crystals will have six facets. Each has its own gifts and magic. I've found six-sided quartz crystals with a straight, flat terminator. If viewed from one side, the termination appears as a point. The top appears as a straight line when rotated 90 degrees. Whereas a true point is a sharpened pencil, think of this type of termination as being more of a "broad brush."

Meditation Crystals—Connector to Spiritual

Quartz Meditation Crystal (with 7 sides marked)

A meditation crystal is a natural quartz crystal with a terminating point and with three faces, or facets, having seven sides. Usually, the three seven-sided faces are larger than the other three, which are triangular in shape.

This configuration offers an enhanced energy flow to the third-eye and crown chakras, hence the association with meditation and connection to the spiritual. The three heptagons (seven-sided shapes) connect your meditations with the sacred number seven.

Vogel Crystals—Energy Collectors and Laser Focusers

Vogel Crystals

Vogel-cut® crystals, conceived through channeled wisdom received by Marcel Vogel, are pure quartz crystal mechanically rendered into mathematically precise facets with termination points. As function follows form, the number of facets on the Vogel-cut® crystal determines its resonant frequency and best application. The energetic potential of this form increases as more sides are added to the crystal.

Marcel Vogel suggests four- sided crystals are more suited to physical treatments, six-sided crystals address more emotional/mental issues, while the eight-sided crystal penetrates to deeper challenges on a mental/causal energetic level.[1]

I've had some very profound and demonstrable results with Vogel-cut® crystals. (See chapter 11) The user needs to be very clear in their intentions, as the Vogel-cut® crystal consolidates the energy field generated by your body, mind and spirit into a concentrated, laser-like force.

Essentially, energy enters the crystal from your hand and the intent of your mind. This energy "binds" and spirals within the crystal, resonating off each facet. The energy travels towards and out of the point(s) with laser-like precision. The Vogel-cut® crystal generates this coherent energy due to the Law of Form, which is why different facet configurations potentially possess different resonate frequencies.

Essentially, a Vogel-cut® crystal amplifies your intentions. Remember, you are a channel for God/Spirit/Source healing energy through your body, mind and spirit. Through your intentions as a clear and perfect channel, you become a conduit for the Universal Life Force energy.

Rounded Gemstones—Gentle Reminders

Natural River Rock (L) polished and Tumbled Quartz (M) and Lapis

Unless a rock has spent years in a flowing river, most rounded minerals/gemstones are mechanically tumbled and polished. Some crystals with the hexagonal termination have rounded "bottoms," which are used for massage and relaxation.

Rounded gemstones attract a softer, more subtle energy. This shape connects you with a specific energy signature and is optimum for carrying or wearing for therapeutic purposes. A small, round and flat gemstone acts as a "touchstone" you can keep in your pocket or around your environment.

For a gentle, relaxing energy bath, use seven small flat rounded gemstones associated with each chakra. Find a comfortable surface where you can lie down, undisturbed for at least 15 minutes. Place the stones on this surface such that when you lie down on the stones, each is aligned with the chakras on your body. Place the crown chakra stone slightly above your head.

You may lie down and place each stone on your front, again aligning each stone with its corresponding chakra. The crown chakra stone may be placed above the brow (third-eye chakra) or above your head.

Remember to take deep "belly breaths" while enjoying the stones' energy. You might want to set a timer for 15 minutes. When you arise, slowly roll over to your side and raise your body gently. Thank the elementals for this peaceful experience.

Spheres —Gentle Energy Circulator

Turquoise and Coral Malas

Spheres are another human-fashioned shape of a mineral. From very small beads to large diameter crystal balls, spheres radiate a flowing, balanced energy. Like Mother Earth's spheroid shape, gemstone spheres have a north and south "pole" with the energy moving in a figure-eight (∞) flow or a swirl pattern.

Generally, smaller spheres work best when they are stranded together. When in at least a 16" stand, the energy gently undulates through the strand. Beads of a 6 mm diameter yield a gentle effect, while 8 mm is the ideal diameter for a strand. 10 mm beads radiate an even stronger energy as, in a strand, their influence is multiplied.

Using a strand of spheres is an ancient spiritual practice. Hindus and Buddhists incorporate a string of prayer beads in their spiritual practice called *Japa*. A *Japa* Mala is made from 108 beads, though other numbers are also used. The beads are often 8 MM gemstones, such as quartz variants like tiger's-eye. Malas help in focus and keeping count while reciting, chanting or mentally repeating a mantra. A rosary serves a similar function for prayer.

An advantage to a strand of spheres is that different gemstones can be combined in a strand to create an energetic "prescription." In the next chapter, I describe how to choose and combine crystals or gemstones for energy work.

Rough cuts—Raw Form

Natural Raw form Rose Quartz

Rough cuts of minerals appear in their native form, i.e. the mineral hasn't been polished, shaped or cut. I find such examples to have lots of "personality" and raw, unstructured energy. Used in a room, rough cuts help purify and energize the environment. I've found a smooth-bottom rough cut great for massaging tissues. Consider these gems as untouched by mechanical intervention—a pure energy form of the mineral.

Pyramid Power

Pyramid shape cut from Rose Quartz

The pyramid is the most perfect structure known to humans. Contemporary scientists are still attempting to analyze and explain this enigma. Ancient philosophies and mystery schools possess the knowledge and have used the powers inherent in the pyramid.

A pyramid acts as an antenna. It receives and transmits Bioenergy, the primordial cosmic energy, the "stuff" that forms all within our Universe.

Resonating with this energy of the pyramid can transform our lives. The presence of a pyramid in a home harmonizes the atmosphere and stabilizes interpersonal relationships of those living within as the pyramid neutralizes negative energies.

The imbalance of our aura, i.e. our bioplasmic body, can cause illnesses in the physical body. Meditation in the presence of a pyramid restores the balance and brings us to a state of deep and invigorating consciousness.

Pyramids cut from stones possess a greater capacity for condensing Universal Life Force energy. A stone-cut pyramid kept in your energy field will attract higher octave energies. To recharge the pyramid's condensing abilities, place the pyramid stone in the sun with one side facing magnetic north.

Experiments with pyramids cut from rose quartz demonstrate the power of this geometric form to enhance the human energy field. Through the aura and chakra imaging system, we have shown that a pyramid placed on the head enhances and extends the auric field. In some instances, the aura size doubled. When the auric field is strong and cohesive, it vibrates at a higher frequency, therefore attracting higher octave energies.

Pyramids cut from stone can be used for specific purposes. To awaken and strengthen the third eye chakra, lie on your back in a comfortable position. Place the pyramid between the eyebrows on your forehead. Keep it there for five minutes every day or for ten minutes three times per week. If you want to sit up, tape the pyramid to the same area of your forehead.

Holding a pyramid in your hands for ten minutes increases your personal magnetism. Start with one hand holding it then, after five minutes, change hands. Women need to start with the pyramid in their left hand, men in their right.

With a smaller pyramid shaped stone, ten minutes time and some tape, you can improve your communications and intuition. Tape the pyramid to your right arm to expand how you communicate and to your left arm to enhance your intuition. In both instances, tape near the shoulder on the outside below the shoulder joint.

Your meditation practice is enriched by placing the pyramid on the top of your head, aligning with the crown chakra. The "sweet" spot is over the fontanelle—the area of the skull that is soft in an infant and later closes as the skull bones mature.

---

[1] http://www.vogelcrystals.net/questions.htm

Notes:

How Do I Know What Crystals to Use?

"Energy work is priceless. It makes every day extraordinary and transforms the mundane to the holy."~Silvia Hartmann

How Do I Know What Crystal/Gemstones to Use?

When beginning to incorporate crystals and gemstones in your energy work, start with clear quartz crystals. Having seven small crystals with pointed ends will help you to clear and balance all your chakras.

Clear quartz attracts all seven of the prismatic colors to the physical body. Quartz energizes the entire aura, attracting the life force energy to disharmonious areas of your body, mind and spirit. This effect brings your being into balance and aligns you with Mother Earth.

As you expand your awareness and explore what works for your HES, you might introduce other gemstones into your life. The provided charts and tables are guidelines based on ancient wisdom and a lineage of usage. Use this information as a starting point in your journey. Pay attention and keep notes. Ask questions and get feedback if you work with others.

Each crystal/gemstone is associated with one of the seven major chakra energy centers. Some of the gemstones are balancing, or calming (yin) while others tend to be more energizing (yang).

Stones that are silicates—derived from silica—are denoted. Since the piezoelectric properties of silica enhance energy transmissions, I prefer to work with these gemstones when my intention is to emit, transmit or draw out energy. Quartz, the purest silicate in mineral form, is my first choice for this type of energy work. Silicate minerals such as topaz and tourmaline also possess this property to focus and transmit energy.

As you review the chakra/gemstone tables, you may see overlaps on some of the gemstone/chakra associations. As a basic guideline, using the "Law of Correspondence," select a gemstone associated with an energy/thought you intend to attract or an area of your life you chose to heal.

Like people, gemstones have their own personality and energy signature. Unless dyed, naturally occurring gemstones range in color and quality. Personally, I don't recommend using dyed crystals in energy work. If you feel a color is required, use a clear quartz crystal and introduce the color via a silk scarf or fresh flowers.

As a guideline, a paler stone—more of a tint—has softer, more receptive yin characteristics. A stone with a brighter hue tends more towards assertive/yang energy. Warm colors—red, orange and yellow—are more active/yang whereas the electric colors—blue, indigo and violet—are more calming and yin. Green balances in the mid-point. A warmer, emerald green is more powerful and energizing than a sea-green aqua.

Aventurine, associated with both the heart and throat chakras, ranges from light green to a dark, emerald green. The dark green is excellent for physical healing while the light green tint provides a gentle, balancing spiritual effect on the aura.

Most energetic therapies require a multi-faceted approach, which is why I recommend a combination of stones with an energetic signature in mind. As well, certain gemstones, while beneficial, may be too overwhelming to wear by themselves.

Garnet is an example of this—red is very energizing and powerful—great for stimulating and grounding. However, in concentrated dosages, it can overpower and "burn out" quickly. Many of us like pepper in our food—it spices up a dish and adds variety to the meal. Yet, we wouldn't think of just eating pepper. So it is with the red gemstones—generally the gemstone is more beneficial if combined and balanced with other gems and metals.

If your intention is to have a "no holds barred" energy jolt, then, by all means wear a solid garnet/ruby necklace! Just pay attention to your energy with the awareness that this red gemstone can be over stimulating if worn above the heart level. Garnet, when worn as a necklace or earrings, may cause you to develop a nervous or tense feeling. If so it is best to remove the gemstones and place in a hip pocket or around your ankle.

When I work with clients in an Aura and Chakra Imaging session, I look at the overall energy levels of their chakras. Often, two or three chakras will show a low "volume" of their energy levels. For example, the root, heart and crown chakras are all at a 20% level as illustrated in this graph (below) from an aura and chakra imaging session.

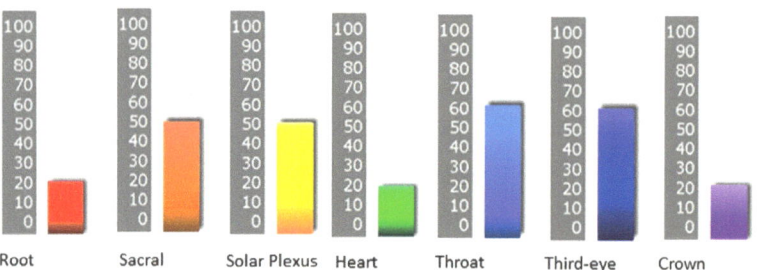

After some discussion, I determine the individual has been "burning the candle at both ends" (low root and crown chakras) at a job she doesn't love (heart chakra). I suggest garnet (root), rose quartz (heart) and amethyst (crown) in round, flat stones or spheres. This combination brings gentle, calming energy, enabling my client to reconnect with spirit and her heart on a physical level.

To attract prosperity and self-confidence (solar plexus chakra) I recommend citrine in a crystal point, a smooth flat-round or a sphere. If I want to direct this energy to a specific area, I'd use a point.

If the solar plexus chakra is over-active and expressing lower octave energies, I suggest amethyst or clear quartz to raise the vibratory level to a more altruistic level. Violet is the complementary color of yellow, both in the additive (light) and subtractive (chemistry) color wheel.

If I am using gemstones for a full chakra clearing, balancing and alignment, I prefer to select a stone for each chakra from the same mineral composition family. (Refer to Chapter 15, Chakra Gemstone Correspondences Guide)

Essentially, choose a quartz mineral for each chakra or a silicate mineral or a calcite, etc. Because gemstones from the same mineral family have the identical underlying geometric structure, I have found these "family" members are better able to communicate and resonate with each other. Since they naturally calibrate their interrelated energy flow, I find these "families" entrain your chakras' energy in a similar manner.

Remember to monitor your energy when using gemstones. (I discuss "testing" your energy fields in the next chapter.) Like many things in life, what was beneficial yesterday may prove ineffective today.

Recently, a client came to me for an aura and chakra imaging session. Part way through my analysis, she exclaimed, "I'm wearing this crystal energy device! Will this impact my chakras and aura?" Being curious myself, I invited her to remove this device, place it in her purse and walk around for a few minutes before we took another look. Ten minutes later, she was amazed to see a much stronger, cohesive energy field and much brighter, rounder chakras.

At some level, you have the capability of manifesting anything through your power of thought. However, this 3rd density, or three-dimensional, life throws enough challenges in your way that you "forget" you have this innate ability. Using gemstones assists you as a reminder of how and where you wish to focus your thoughts and energy.

Notes:

10

Selecting Programming And using crystals

"We live as ripples of energy in the vast ocean of energy." ~Deepak Chopra

Selecting, Programming and Using Crystals

Besides selecting a crystal for a specific energetic property you want to evoke, sometimes you acquire a crystal as you are meant to have it. You might be wandering through a shop and a crystal just "pops" out at you. Instantly, you feel a connection—an energy exchange.

When working with clients, I'm often asked what crystals are best for balancing or enhancing their aura and chakras. Although I can give them some specific suggestions, I advise them to wander around a store selling crystals and pay attention to any one that pops out at them. Usually I suggest they hold their hand over that crystal. If the energy from that crystal feels "hotter" than adjacent one, then that's the "one" for them.

Before using your crystal, I suggest cleaning it and then programming it for your energy work. Remember, your new crystal has taken a bit of a trip getting to you from Mother Earth, passing through several hands on its journey.

As you clean your crystal, mentally set the intention that any lower octave energies be dissolved and released back into Mother Earth. Perform the cleansing with love. To energetically clear or clean your crystal do one of the following:

1. Run lukewarm tap water over it. Dry thoroughly.

2. Place the crystal on a bed of sea salt or pink Himalayan salt (no water) for at least four hours.

3. Wash the crystal in sea water (or water with sea salt or pink Himalayan salt added). Rinse with clear tap water and dry thoroughly.

4. Place the crystal on the soil at the base of either an indoor or outdoor plant. Leave overnight.

5. Place the crystal on an amethyst cluster and leave overnight.

Love is the most important ingredient in programming and working with crystals. When you use a crystal, you are creating a relationship between you and the elementals of the mineral kingdom. This relationship, once cultivated, strengthens your physical, mental, emotional and spiritual bodies. Love attunes you to the crystal. Give thanks to Mother Earth and the elementals.

You can program your crystal for a precise purpose, such as a specific energy work like Reiki or reading the Akashic records. You might want to use your crystal for distance healing. Perhaps you just want to work with that crystal's energy to balance your energy and learn more about yourself. Set your intentions and begin by asking the elementals to work with you. You are working together for your mutual highest good. Of course, always include love in your endeavors.

Once you have cleared and programmed your crystal, you don't need to re-clean or reprogram unless going through this process seems "right" to you. As you develop your intuition and inner wisdom, you learn to honor your guidance and know when it is aligned with your highest good.

Using Crystals—Decor

From small specimens to large clusters, crystals come in many sizes and are used in a variety of applications. Large clusters or single points bring energy into a room—a large amethyst cluster purifies the room's energies and radiates peaceful energy.

Placement in a room is important for a larger crystal's effectiveness. In décor, crystals with plants are a good marriage of energies. Reception areas, entry foyers and living rooms are candidates for crystals. A water fountain with crystals, especially by the front entrance or door, cleans the energy of all who enter and, according to Feng Shui, brings prosperity into the building/home.

Some individuals may not be able to sleep with crystals in their room. Crystals with a calming, peaceful energy signature can also enhance rest. Pay attention to the overall effect a crystal has on a living area. Basically, it's all about your intention with the crystal.

Using Crystals and Your Human Energy Field

If you are a novice with crystals, I recommend you work with another person who can "read" how the crystal affects your human energy field—your aura. Doing so is part of your learning process so you can effectively use crystals for your personal growth.

Several ways to learn how crystals' energy impacts your aura:

1. Aura and Chakra Imaging—Often, I'm asked by my clients to "test" a specific crystal or gemstone and see how it impacts their aura and chakras. (For more information about Aura Photos and Chakra Imaging, please visit my website at www.ChakraCoach.me). We usually do a before image and then introduce the stone in question into their energy field. Sometimes, the client's field is impacted immediately. Often, the effects are more subtle and can take several hours to record a noticeable change.

2. Muscle testing—Applied Kinesiology (AK) is a muscle testing technique. Muscle testing uses your body's muscles to give a "true/false" reading. In AK, a muscle that tests strong equals a "true" reading whereas a muscle that tests weak indicates a "false" reading. AK presupposes your body intrinsically "knows" what is beneficial and what is harmful for you. Through AK calibration, you learn what is "good" and "true" for your well-being and what is detrimental (false) for you.

Using AK, you can determine if a crystal is for the highest good of your energy system. First, hold the crystal over your breast bone (sternum), just below the notch at the shoulder line. Ask "Is this (crystal) good for me" while testing your reference muscle. If you get a "true" reading, then hold the crystal over your navel. Ask "Do I need this crystal now" while testing the muscle. If yes, then at this point in time, you will get great benefits from working with the crystal.

3. Dowsing—A pendulum, if you are familiar with its use, helps determine if a crystal or gemstone is beneficial for you at this time. Dowsing does take some practice for proficiency and accuracy. In some respects, it's similar to AK as you look for "yes/no" validation. Hold the pendulum over the crystal and mentally ask, "Is this crystal for my highest good?" Then ask, "Do I need this crystal now?"

With both AK and dowsing, I continue asking a few more questions eliciting yes/no answers, such as:

- Do I need to wear the crystal? If yes, then go through a list of possibilities.
- If negative to wearing, ask how to use, i.e. in meditation, in my bedroom, on my office desk, etc.
- How long does my body need the crystal in its aura? Minutes? Hours? Days? Weeks?

Whatever method you employ, remember to keep testing the stone's ongoing effectiveness. Just as you (hopefully) wouldn't take a laxative every day, certain gemstones are not to be worn 24/7.

Keep a journal of your experiences with crystals and gemstones. Pay attention to how you feel, the level of your energy and any physical sensations. Note if you feel spacey, have a headache or are dizzy. If you experience any of these symptoms, immediately distance yourself from the crystal. Wash your hands, take several deep "belly breaths," walk outside or dance/move around. Sometimes, other factors in your life besides the crystal may have precipitated these symptoms. If you record such events, then you will know if it's a one-time occurrence or a characteristic of the crystal.

Crystals don't need to be mounted in jewelry to be effective. Place the crystal in a small bag and wear against your body. In this manner, you can pin it to undergarments in a specific area.

Single crystals terminated with a point are effective at directing energy flows, although you need to pay attention to where the point is aimed. Pointed down towards your feet relieves stress. Yet, if left in that position too long, you could feel light-headed and drained. Once you feel de-stressed, point the crystal towards your head to draw energy from the Earth.

Relieving Pain

If you are experiencing pain, place an appropriate crystal in your left hand and place your right hand on the area with pain. Breathe the color of the crystal in, directing towards your right hand and the area of concern. If you entire body aches, place your right hand with the crystals on your solar plexus area and your left hand on your head. Take several deep "belly breaths," directing the energy through the crystal.

Energy Balance

When your physical body is depleted of energy, use five single-pointed quartz crystals to balance your energy. Find a space to lie down and remain undisturbed for 15 to 30 minutes. First, you will position the crystals to channel off non-resourceful energies, clearing the space for attracting higher octave energies.

Place one crystal above your head, one on each side by your hands and one below each foot. Align the crystals pointing, at first, outwards, i.e. away from your body in a pattern where the crystal at your head points to magnetic north. Breathe with "belly breaths" until you feel any negative energy has left you. Then, reverse the points of the crystals so that they are pointed towards your body. This directs the higher octave energies to your energy field.

Quick energizer with Crystals

This quick energizer uses quartz crystals to enhance the flow of life force energies, which enter the body through the feet, hands, medulla oblongata (base of the neck) and the crown of the head.

You will need:

1. Six quartz crystals with single point terminations. Use sizes that will comfortably fit on the soles of the feet, hands, neck and crown.

2. A partner to place the crystals

3. A comfortable place where you can lie on your stomach. A massage table with a face donut is ideal to keep your face open for breathing. You can also roll up several towels to cradle your face on a bed or the floor.

Lie down on your stomach with your face down, palms turned up and feet stretched out so that your soles face up.

Have your partner place the crystals as follows: (diagram on next page)

- On your left palm, the crystal points up towards your shoulder
- On your right palm, the crystal points towards your fingertips, away from your body
- On your left sole, the crystal points up towards your leg and back (Hint—to keep the crystal in place on the soles, wear socks made of a natural fiber, such as cotton, bamboo or wool, and place the crystal inside the sock)
- On your right sole, the crystal points towards your toes, away from your body
- On the back of your neck (at the base of where your head meets your neck), the crystal points towards the head
- Just above your head, the crystal points towards the crown (the top of your head)

Once the crystals are placed, remain in that position for about 10 minutes. Remember to take slow, steady "belly breaths" while in this position. Attune your thoughts to your Higher Self and the Universal Life Force Energy.

When you are finished, ask your partner to remove the crystals. Slowly roll over on your side and gently raise your body from the bed. Take a few deep "belly breaths" and give thanks to the crystals for assisting you in this process.

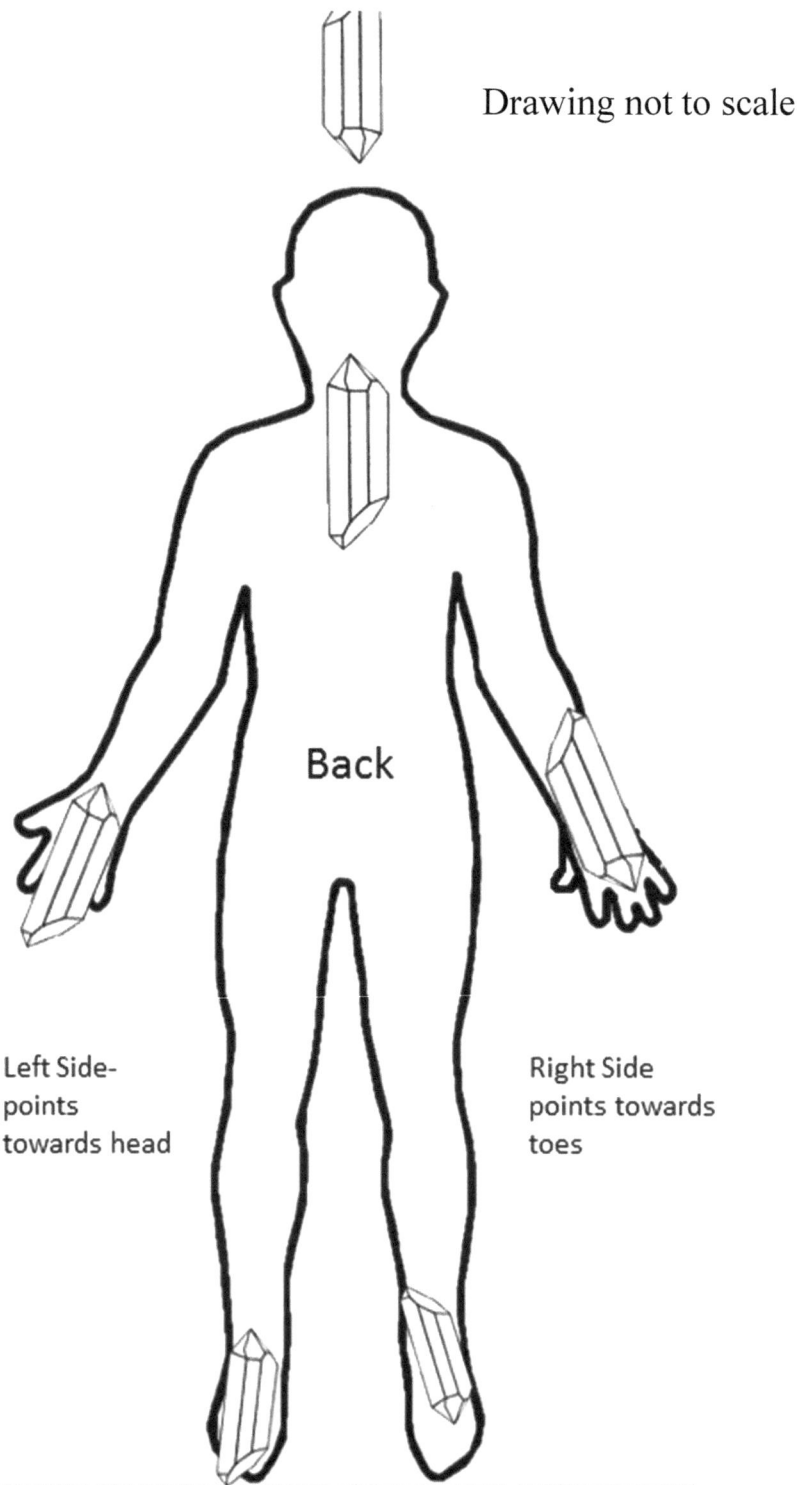

Balancing the Seven Major Chakras

"The energy of the mind is the essence of life." ~Aristotle

Balancing the Seven Major Chakras

In my Aura and Chakra Imaging – 7 Keys to Unlock Your Energy Blueprint class, I'm frequently asked, "Do crystals help to clear, activate and balance my chakras?"

It depends on a number of factors.

We explore this question in my class, as the participants play with a variety of crystals while they watch their energy field and chakras shift.

Over time, we've witnessed a gamut of responses. Sometimes, crystals have little or no impact on the person's energy field and chakras. Sometimes, a crystal acts as a mild "tonic" for the chakras. What may produce results for one person does nothing for another in the immediate.

Occasionally, a crystal introduced into an individual's energy field will have a dramatic impact. On my website, I posted a video excerpt from one aura and chakra class session demonstrating the impact of a Vogel-cut® crystal on the human energy field, specifically on the heart chakra.

In this video, there is a great spiritual expansion of the heart chakra witnessed when the 12 sided, double pointed Vogel-cut crystal was held in the right hand of my student. The intense blue color indicates much heart energy pouring forth, expressing a deep spiritual healing.

After a point in time, this energy became so intense I removed the Vogel crystal from the student's hand, partially to prevent an overload of the aura and chakra imaging system. Yes, the person was ready for a replenishment of their spirit. In this case, the Vogel crystal was probably the tipping point for the catharsis. It was very a profound and healing experience for my student — to know how to activate the heart energy, to become aware of this energy, and to go forth in the world, radiating love and compassion.

Now, I have introduced this same Vogel crystal into other's energy fields and have observed reactions varying from minimal to a nice, consistent balancing of all the Chakras. I have seen the same person using the same crystal on two different occasions with two different results.

Why the inconsistencies?

You are a unique individual and your chakras and human energy field (HEF) are dynamic and constantly changing. Crystals act as a reminder for your chakras to stay in balance. When you pay attention to your body, mind and spirit, you will know if crystal energies would benefit your overall energy balance. You may need to have a crystal or combination of crystals in your energy field for several minutes, hours, or days.

To quote from Abraham (Hicks): *"It usually takes about 30 days to change a habit. Not because you need 30 days. You could do it in 68 seconds if you could, once you did it, hold your vibration there, but you have to consciously make that decision."*

Crystals help you tune into and hold a desired vibration as well as act as a reminder for your conscious decisions. Becoming aware of what you need to balance your chakras develops your inner wisdom.

Clearing, Awakening and Balancing the Chakras

On a daily basis, you can use a crystal to "tune into" your seven major chakras. I have seen great improvements using the following technique over time. Individuals who pay attention to their energy field and hold the intention of connecting with the high octaves of each chakra have the most significant results.

The best crystal for this practice is a clear quartz crystal, 2" to 3" in length with a single terminated point The single point focuses the energy and clear quartz is the master facilitator for this use.

As you practice this technique, you might notice sensations. I have listed several potential experiences for each chakra, more for reassurances than for what will happen. You may experience one, two or all of them. You may not have any. You may have other sensations. I invite you to write these experiences in a journal after you complete the process.

Find a quiet, undisturbed area where you feel safe to relax for about 15 to 30 minutes. If you can, stand tall as you can better focus the crystal in that position. Sit tall on a chair if standing for 10 to 15 minutes is a challenge. Begin by taking three deep "belly breaths."

You will start with the crown chakra and work towards the root. Hold your crystal at all times in your right (energy sending) hand, with the crystal point aimed towards the body. Wherever "rotate the crystal" is mentioned, move your hand in a clockwise, circular direction, holding the crystal fixed in your hand. Close your eyes.

Crown Chakra

Hold the crystal a few inches above the top of your head. Keeping your eyes closed, rotate the crystal gently in small circles, moving clockwise. While rotating your crystal, imagine a white light emanating from the crystal and entering the top of your head. Continue rotating and imagining white light for 10 seconds to a minute—you will "know" when to stop as your hand may feel heavy. If you experience any discomfort or dizziness, discontinue the rotation.

Relax and lower your arm. Remain quiet for a few moments. Note any sensations or experiences. Possible crown chakra experiences:

- Discomfort
- Heat at the "point of entry" of the white light
- Tingling sensation
- Flashing colored light
- Patterns and designs

Patterns and designs may not appear until you have been practicing this technique for a while. Make notes of any images or patterns even if you don't, at first, make sense of them.

Third Eye Chakra

Hold your crystal about 3" to 4" away from your forehead, angled down slightly so it points at the area between your eye brows. Keeping your eyes closed, rotate the crystal slowly and gently in a clockwise direction for 30 seconds to several minutes. Lower your hand and relax, allowing the sensations to continue for a few moments longer.

Possible third eye chakra experiences:

- light "stabbing" sensation in the forehead area
- Heat in the forehead
- Circle of light
- Heaviness above nose or below eyes

Throat Chakra

Hold your crystal no more than 6" from the throat chakra i.e. pointed at the base of the throat. Ensure the crystal in held in a horizontal position, parallel to the floor. Close your eyes and imagine a ray of pure white light emanating from the crystal and entering your throat at the position of this chakra.

If your hand "feels" like it wants to rotate let it gently do so. Otherwise, keep your hand and crystal focused on your throat. Remain in that position for 1 to 2 minutes. Lower your hand and relax, allowing the sensations to continue for a few moments longer.

Possible throat chakra experiences:

- Heat
- Desire to cough
- Feeling the body's "engine" is racing
- Increased energy
- Expansiveness around throat

Heart Chakra

Hold your crystal 3" to 4" from your body, pointed towards your upper chest, slightly above your breasts and aimed at the middle of your chest. Keep the crystal parallel with the floor. Close your eyes and imagine a vibrant white light coming from the crystal and entering your body at the level of your heart chakra. Concurrently, imagine a pure white light emanating from your heart chakra and linking with the light coming from the crystal.

Often, I imagine this exchange and movement of light between the crystal and my heart form a figure eight ∞.

If your hand "feels" like it wants to rotate let it gently do so. Otherwise, keep your hand and crystal focused on your heart chakra. Remain in that position for 1 to 2 minutes. Lower your hand and relax, allowing the sensations to continue for a few moments longer.

Possible heart chakra experiences:

- Tingling sensation
- Warmth in chest
- Tears
- Joy

Solar Plexus Chakra

Hold your crystal 3" to 4" from your body, pointed towards your diaphragm/solar plexus chakra. Keep the crystal parallel with the floor. Close your eyes and imagine a vibrant white light coming from the crystal and entering your body at the level of your solar plexus chakra.

If your hand "feels" like it wants to rotate let it gently do so in a slow, wide circle. Otherwise, keep your hand and crystal focused on your solar plexus chakra. Remain in that position for 1 to 2 minutes. Lower your hand and relax, allowing the sensations to continue for a few moments longer.

At first, you may not experience any sensations in this chakra. The solar plexus chakra can hold tensions and sometimes is very protective of old programs and stories.

Possible solar plexus experiences:

- Throbbing or pulsating
- Feeling of heat
- Release of tension from spine

Sacral Chakra

Hold your crystal 2" to 3" from your body, pointed slightly downward towards the area slightly below your navel. Close your eyes and rotate the crystal gently in a clockwise direction. At the same time, imagine a pure white light entering your body at the sacral chakra and then radiating outwards from that point, like the ripples on a pond created by dropping a pebble in the water. Imagine this light filling the surrounding area.

Remain in that position for 1 to 2 minutes. Lower your hand and relax, allowing the sensations to continue for a few moments longer.

Possible sacral chakra experiences:

- Little or no reaction
- Warmth
- Tingling in the area of the chakra
- Relaxation of the spine
- Serenity of the mind
- Warmth spreading throughout the body

Root Chakra

Hold your crystal 2" to 3" from your body, pointed slightly downward towards the area at the base of your spine. Close your eyes and imagine a bright white light entering the body at that single point. Hold the crystal steady when working on the root chakra. Do not rotate it.

Remain in that position for 1 to 2 minutes. Lower your hand and relax, allowing the sensations to continue for a few moments longer.

Possible root chakra experiences:

- Heat at the point of focus
- Spreading of heat throughout your body
- Muscle relaxation in lower body
- Release of tension in your body

When you are complete with this process, take a minute to note any experiences or sensations. You may feel totally relaxed. You might have a few other sensations.

Take three deep "belly breaths" and express gratitude and thanks to your crystal and chakras. If you experience any deep emotional or cathartic releasing, you may want to clean your crystal using one of the methods previously described.

12

Putting It All Together

"In a crystal we have clear evidence of the existence of a formative life principle, and though we cannot understand the life of a crystal, it is nonetheless a living being."~Nikola Tesla

Putting It All Together

By now, you probably have read and absorbed the information about color and crystals. Hopefully, you have read *Chakra Mastery: 7 Keys to Discover Your Inner Wisdom* and are on the path.

I'm an advocate of personal sovereignty. Remember, success is an inside job. Pay attention to your inner world in order to effect changes in your outer world. As well, elements from your outer world can help you get in touch with your inner world. This is where colors and crystals enter into the picture.

The information, charts and tables in this book present a starting point for your personal research. How, then, do you put "it" all together?

Be a detective and look for clues. First, check out your physical body. Review the areas of the body corresponding to each chakra as presented in *Chakra Mastery*. The chakras' effect on the physical body is strong. Perhaps the physical body shapes itself around the chakras, as they are the matrix for your physical manifestation. For example, a poor energetic connection through the root chakra may show as skinny legs or bad knees.

- A constricted throat chakra may manifest as a sore throat or chronically tight shoulders.
- An overblown solar plexus chakra might show up as a big tight belly.
- A non-stop talker is probably caught in an over-active, unbalanced throat chakra.
- If you experience butterflies in your stomach, you may need to calm and balance your solar plexus chakra.
- A gut reaction to a situation stems from the emotions held in your sacral chakra.
- "Frogs" in your throat will show up as low energy in your throat chakra.

- A break-up with your significant other or best friend may manifest as "heart-break" in your heart chakra's energy.

- Feeling "spacey" all the time? You might be experiencing an over-active third-eye or crown chakra.

- A pounding in your heart during certain situations points to challenges with your heart chakra.

- Work related problems usually have their "root" in the first chakra.

Clues also come through your feelings and emotions, often expressed via the words you use. Color analogies—such as seeing red, yellow-bellied, green with envy, feeling blue, true blue, shrinking violet and in the pink—are accurate indicators of what is happening with your chakra system.

Remember, the seven major chakras are inseparably inter-related. An imbalance in one chakra may affect the one(s) above and/or the ones below.

Fear (root chakra) and guilt (sacral chakra) cut off self-confidence (solar plexus). If you live in fear and the past—guilt—then you lack the foundation for taking charge of your life. Choices are made based on what you deem to be safe rather than what is best for your personal growth.

Low self-esteem may arise when wires cross between the sacral and solar plexus chakras. Often, you look outside of yourself for validation of self. You might look to other relationships - family, friends, and lovers - to affirm your "right to be here." Through an emotional imprint, you might perceive that these relationships serve as your "correctness" compass. The sacral chakra, or 2nd chakra, expresses this energy of how you relate to others on an emotional level. As well, the energetic blueprint of this 2nd chakra contains the dynamics of your creativity, sexuality, and the giving and receiving of spiritual, mental, and physical pleasure.

Energetically, a lack of self-worth can also occur when the "wires" are crossed between the solar plexus chakra and the sacral chakra. In this scenario, you do not differentiate between your relationships with others vs. your relationship with self. You look to others to validate self, and, in the process, give away your personal power. This leads to an unhealthy relationship with "self" and an eroded self-worth. When this energetic condition occurs behaviors manifest that range from self-destructive conduct to wanting to over-control all aspects of your life, including the actions of others.

On a physical level, weight challenges may result from imbalances in the 2nd sacral chakra (compulsive behavior), the solar plexus chakra (poor food assimilation) and the throat chakra (thyroid—regulator of metabolism) plus overstressed adrenals (root chakra).

As with any team, when one chakra is compromised, the other team members either take up the "slack" or overcompensate for the low energy of the offending member. This is why you need to pay attention to your Human Energy System and be proactive when you sense one of your team members needs assistance. This is why I recommend regular clearing and balancing of ALL your major chakras.

When your third eye is activated and strong and your chakras are balanced, your "inner tuition"—intuition—guides you to situations beneficial to your personal growth.

A strong functioning third eye paired with your solar plexus chakra is a powerful partnership. If you listen to your intuition, your sense of self-power will be strong. You honor your personal power when you pay attention to your intuition.

The interplay between your sacral and heart chakras reflects your inter-personal relationships and how you feel emotionally about them. If you are caring and compassionate in relationships, then both chakras are resonating to higher octave vibrations.

Co-dependency could arise if both of these chakras are vibrating at lower octave energies. You may not have set the proper boundaries of love for others versus love for self in your heart chakra. Over-giving (heart chakra) in relationships with others (sacral chakra) often results in relying on others for your emotional validation.

Envy results when both the heart and solar plexus chakras are vibrating at lower octave energies. Essentially, you have made a judgment (solar plexus) that you are less than another plus you are not loving yourself or accepting self (heart chakra).

Basically, if you experience any of the lower octave energies associated with one or more of your chakras, then pay attention to those areas of your life. Ask yourself:

1) "Am I feeling depleted in this area at this point in time?"

2) "Is this an area of my life I desire to enhance?"

3) " Is what I'm experiencing an ongoing theme in my life?"

4) "Do I think I have _____ (my life, my relationships, etc.) together then suddenly, _____ (anger, jealousy, etc.) rears up its ugly head?"

If you answered "yes" to either question #1 or # 2 above, then look to the chakra's archetypal color. Use this color to vitalize the energy—connect with the higher vibrational frequencies—and attract this energy into your life. If you also want to use a crystal or gemstone, select one from the table associated with that chakra.

For example, if you wanted to attract more creative energy into your life, then you evoke the sacral chakra's higher vibrations. Since orange resonates with this chakra, introduce this color into your environment. Remember, each color possesses a gamut of energies in hue, tone, tint and shade. You don't have to dress in pumpkin orange—think peach tints, rust shades or subtle tones. Bring fun orange accessories into your life, such as pens, lamps, mouse pads or pillows. Pick one or more gemstones from the sacral chakra chart and wear.

If you responded "yes" to either question #3 or #4 above, then look to the chakra's archetypal color and find the complementary color on the color wheel. Remember, if using light, use the additive color wheel. If using objects or color breathing, use the subtractive color wheel. If you want to use a crystal or gemstone, select one from the table associated with the color's corresponding chakra.

For example, if you find you have self-confidence issues (solar plexus chakra—yellow) then look to the complementary color of yellow, which is violet. Violet corresponds to the crown chakra. Amethyst embodies the crown chakra's energies.

Perhaps you find certain situations where you lack self-confidence, such as public speaking. On that occasion, wear violet, have violet flowers on the dais. Wear an amethyst or have one in your area.

Evoking the vibrational frequencies of the chakra's complementary color balances and re-energizes that chakra. Why? Essentially, you are "pulling" this chakra's energy out of its current energy pattern to create a figure-eight (∞) movement. Once this movement achieves momentum, the chakra begins to reconnect with its higher octave energies. You are reestablishing your yin/yang balance within this energy center by reaching out to its complementary color.

Quick Tips for Success

1. Review the archetypal energies for each chakra in Chapter 13.

2. Look at the Higher Octave and Lower Octave expressions in Chapter 13 for the selected chakra.

3. Note the archetypal color of this chakra. Refer to Chapter 14 for color information.

4. Decide if you want to a) attract or amplify this archetypal energy or b) clear and balance

    a. If attract or amplify, then use the archetypal color

    b. If clear and balance, then use the complementary color

5. Select a crystal/gemstone from Chapter 15 based on your choice in Step #4 above.

    a. If attracting or amplifying, then use a crystal/gemstone from the ones listed for that chakra.

    b. If clearing and balancing, then:

        i. Match the complementary color with its archetypal chakra;

        ii. Select a crystal/gemstone associated with this chakra, i.e. if the complementary color is violet, select a crystal from the crown chakra list.

Note: When working with the heart chakra's complementary color, start with either pink, which is a tint of red, or magenta, the spectral complement of green. I find these complements to green gentler and more effective when working with the heart chakra.

When working with a specific chakra, remember to balance all your chakras with a crystal chakra balance (presented in chapter 11) or use the many Playercises offered in *Chakra Mastery: 7 Keys to Discover Your Inner Wisdom*. Doing this integrates your specific work into your entire Human Energy System.

Notes:

13

The Chakras

"The chakras sing your personal song, echoing your life's experiences."
~Carolyn White

YOUR CHAKRAS / ENERGY CENTERS KEY ASPECTS

Root/Base/Red

The "root" of your energy on the physical plane and material reality, this chakra is the center of manifestation and the place from which passion flows. Your "right livelihood," home and money. Self-Awareness.

Sacral/Orange

The sacral chakra reflects creativity, sociability, emotional life and sexuality. This chakra is the position from which you reach out, expand and relate to others. Self-Respect.

Solar Plexus/Yellow

This chakra rules mental activity and is the center of your ego and personal power. It regulates the life force in the body, giving energy to your dreams and goals, allowing you to take action. Self-Worth.

Heart/Green

Your Heart is the center of teaching and healing, the chakra of compassion, as well as the meeting place for body, mind and spirit. Balance and connection to nature is found here. Self-Love.

Throat/Blue

This chakra governs the ability to express ideas and to speak your truth clearly. The throat is all about clear communication, inspiration and artistic expression. Self-Expression.

Third Eye/Brow/Indigo-Violet

Your "third eye" center is the seat of intuition and spiritual will. Here is the energy for connecting ideas and developing a "picture" of the world. It is an idealistic place representing your imagination and desires. Self-Responsibility.

Crown/ Violet- White

Your Inner Knowledge, enlightenment, connection with higher planes of consciousness and spiritual truth resides in the crown chakra. White in the crown represents the perfect merging of all colors. Self-Knowledge.

Root Chakra

Higher Octave - Master Path

Grounded
Passion
Physical Security
Physical Power
Sexuality/activate ability to create
Courage
Stability, Strength
Vitality, activity
Healthy eating patterns
Sense of Well-being
Calmness
Contentment

Lower Octave - Student Path

Ungrounded
Lack of confidence in your future
Money issues
Lack of physical energy
Suicidal
Aggression
Anxiety, depression
Hostility
Obesity/anorexia nervosa - eating disorders
Stress
Tension
Rage

Sacral Chakra

Higher Octave - Master Path

Creativity
Clear emotions and feelings
Satisfaction
Spontaneity
Sensuality
Healthy Sexuality
Trusting
Faith
Natural healing abilities
Flexibility
Loyalty

Lower Octave - Student Path

Not honoring true nature
Resentfulness
Over-indulgent
Shyness
Loneliness
Multiple partners/relationships
Jealousy
Self-negating
Addictions, substance abuse
Dogmatic
Difficulty in maintaining relationships

Solar Plexus Chakra

Higher Octave - Master Path

Self-Esteem
Discerning
Positive Self-Image
Personal Power
Active Intellect
Independence
Happiness
In touch with your gifts
Alignment with cosmic personal path
Open to new ideas
Healthy Digestion

Lower Octave - Student Path

Self-condemnation
Lack of confidence
People pleaser
Perfectionist
Dependency
Anxiety
Mental stress
Arrogance
Egotistical
Judgmental
Digestive problems

CAROLYN WHITE PHD

Heart Chakra

Higher Octave - Master Path

Compassion
Loving
Caring
Generosity
Selflessness
Healing
Devotion
Nurturing
Balance
Discerning
Acceptance
Healthy Immune System

Lower Octave - Student Path

Paranoid
Hatred
Overly critical
Demanding
Feels sorry for self
Tenseness between shoulders
Co-dependence
Moody
Indecision
Unaware
Grief
Heart and Lung problems

Throat Chakra

Higher Octave - Master Path

Good Communication
Able to express True Self
Inspiration
Contented
Lives in the Present

Musically Inspiring
Open
Artistically Inspiring
Honest
Authentic

Flexible

Lower Octave - Student Path

Poor Communication
Talks too much
Can't express thoughts
Infections - sore throat
Bronchial problems

Cold hands and feet
Arrogant
Dogmatic
Scared
Timid
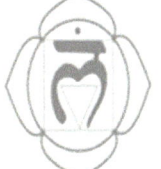
Devious
Manipulative
Inability to hear truth
Stiff neck

Third Eye Chakra

Higher Octave - Master Path

Intuitive
Clear Vision
Creativity
Highly ethical
Non-attachment to material things
In tune to guidance
Charismatic
Inner Wisdom
Clarity of Thought
Telepathy
Visualization
Imagination
Self-Reflection

Lower Octave - Student Path

Paranoid
Dogmatic
Manipulative
Dependence
Undisciplined
Nervousness
Non-Assertive
Over-clouded with thought
Doubt
Recurring Nightmares
Delusions
Eye or facial problems, Headaches

Crown Chakra

Higher Octave - Master Path

Spirituality
Integrated Life
Light-worker Energy
Higher Consciousness Knowledge
Connected to Source
Grounded in Your Life's Purpose
Physically healthy
Enlightened
Altruistic
Transcendence

Lower Octave - Student Path

Indecisive
Flighty
Constant frustration
Boundaries dissolve
Confused
Foggy
No connection with physical body
Ungrounded
Brain Issues
Head issues
Frequent headaches
Psychotic

Notes:

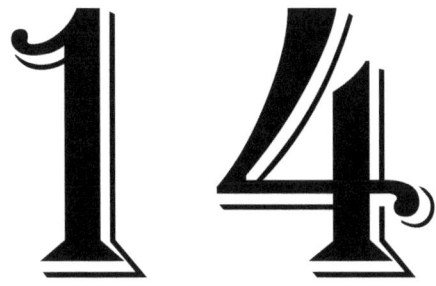

Archetypal Color Energies

*Seven Spectral Colors
*Specific Color Applications

Archetypal Energies of Seven Spectral Colors

Red — Root Chakra

Since red has the slowest vibration rate of all the visible colors, it affects emotions faster than the other spectral colors. Perhaps that is why red is used for stop signs and warning symbols. Red is contraindicated for anger issues and is a disturbing influence for people with mental problems or neuroses.

Red is a physical color. Many chronically ill people need this basic "Hot" energy for healing and alleviating discomfort. They will experience heat entering into the body, which is a quality of the sensation of power going into the spine.

Higher Octave	Lower Octave
Vitality	Fear
Energy	Anxiety
Excitement	Anger
Warmth	Suffering
Strength	Uncontrolled passion
Joy	Lust
Happiness	Warning
Will-Power	Injury
Determination	

Orange — Sacral Chakra

Since many fruits and vegetables are orange or orange-red, this color is associated with nourishment. Horticulturist Luther Burbank discovered orange light speeds up plant growth. In the mineral kingdom, orange signifies attraction of the elements as it works as a cohesive atomic force.

Higher Octave	Lower Octave
Creativity	Analysis Paralysis
Ambition	Nervousness
Analysis	Restlessness
Energetic activity	Disrespect
Pride	
Preservation	
Self-expression	
Confidence	

Yellow — Solar Plexus Chakra

Yellow vegetables and fruits can act as laxatives for the bowel and also calm the nerves. Traditional Chinese Medicine views the Solar Plexus as the center for all digestion.

Higher Octave	Lower Octave
Wisdom	Over-thinking
Logic	Over-critical
Intellect	Perfectionism
Joyfulness	People-pleaser
Cheery	Egocentric
Spiritual wisdom	Cowardice
Compassion (gold)	Prejudice
Creativity	Destructive Domination

Green — Heart Chakra

Green is Mother Nature's color from the green of spring's new life to the deep forest evergreens. It possesses great healing properties and, as the middle of the spectrum, is balancing by nature. Yellow-green stimulates generosity on the mental plane and elimination of toxins and waste on the physical plane. Green creates a space for new possibilities.

Higher Octave	Lower Octave
Soothing	Jealousy
Peaceful	Selfishness
Healing	Laziness
Social	Depressing
Open to change	Envy
Growth	
Balance	
Harmony	

Blue — Throat Chakra

Since the daylight sky is blue, it is often thought of as heavenly consciousness. Tints of blue soothe the passions evoked by red, as well as serve as sedatives. In the tropics, clothing colored tints of blue provide the best protection from the sun's UVA and UVB rays. Blue and green together—aqua or turquoise—are the most healing colors as well as stimulating the highest creativity in music and art.

Higher Octave	Lower Octave
Loyalty	Depression—"The Blues"
Calmness	Smothering
Truth	Uncommunicative
Hope	Withdrawn
Awareness	
Communication	

Indigo — Third Eye Chakra

Some color experts deny the existence of indigo as a spectral color lodged between blue and violet. Like its counterpart third-eye chakra and associated pineal gland, it symbolizes the transmutation of old energies into new spiritual growth. In the realm of the deep blue-violet color lays the eternal, unlimited world of the imagination and inspiration.

Higher Octave	Lower Octave
Ethical Values	Close-minded
Reason combined with intuition	Disillusionment
	Stagnation
Discipline with creativity	Mental Fatigue
Power with Understanding and Knowledge	Frustration
Visionary	

Violet — Crown Chakra

Violet is often associated with the "Crown" heads of Europe as royalty donned violet robes as a symbol of their moral and spiritual authority. Purportedly 19th century composer Richard Wagner composed his greatest works in rooms decorated with violet velvet drapes. The tint of violet, as in a pale orchid, is the vibration of the truth seeker.

Higher Octave	Lower Octave
Prosperity	Pretense
Spirituality	Snobbery
Self-mastery	Deceit
Aspirations	

Reference Tables for Specific Color Applications

Each color's archetypal energies assist with physical, mental and emotional challenges. Following are tables for each of the seven spectral colors, listing areas of life that can benefit from that color's vibration.

As previously detailed, the specified color can be used as a focus for breathing, meditation, color and light therapy or use in your environment.

This guide can help you select a crystal for therapeutic use. Use a crystal or gemstone of the desired color. Please refrain from using a dyed stone.

For all physical conditions, please consult your health care practitioner. Color augments all healing modalities.

Where applicable, I have included comments on the specific areas for each color.

Color Me Healthy Wealthy and Wise

Red is Excellent for:	Comments
Anemia	Links to Bloodstream.
Apathy	Energizes
Arthritis (Rheumatoid)	Helps if not acute or inflammation present.
Arteries	Stimulates Blood flow.
Bladder Infections	Warmth helps manage pain. **Red** cranberry juice.
Blood Pressure (low)	Contraindicated for high blood pressure.
Cancer	With any growth, intelligence within cell has been deprogrammed. **Red** with visualization and imagination can restore energy in cell.
Childbirth	Good for energizing after delivery.
Depletion of Energy	Energizes
Depression	Stimulates to take action.
Digestion	Use when sluggish (**red** check table cloths).
Exhaustion	Re-energizer
Eyeballs	Use if eyes have bluish tinge instead of white.
Fear	Helps motivate if frozen in fear.
Frigidity	Sexual energizer; warmth to lower area of body.
Grounding	Helps ground a person-use with **orange** and **yellow** as well.
Impotence	Sexual energizer; warmth to lower area of body.
Lethargy	Use if lack of vitality along with **orange** and **yellow**.
Male Virility	Helps Deficient sexual drive.
Menstrual Period	Warmth may lessen cramps and pain.
Muscles	Energizes muscles.
Nerves	Helps with patients in shock.
Paralysis	Brings warmth and re-energizes physical body.
Shock	Contraindicated if pain, fear or excitement present.
Skin	Brings warmth and energy.
Sluggish Conditions	Energizes
Stiffness in Joints	Brings warmth and energy.
Warmth	
Vitality	

Orange is Excellent for:	Comments
Addictions (alcohol/drugs)	Decreases Cravings.
Asthma	Use with Indigo as well.
Abdomen (gut feelings)	Helps to release emotion of suspicion and anxiety.
Bladder	Use along with cranberry juice.
Bones (soft)	Associated with lack of calcium.
Breast Milk	Stimulates and increases flow.
Bronchitis	Strengthens lungs.
Colon	Soothes inflammation.
Congestions	Helps relieve thick mucous in sinuses.
Colitis	Soothes inflammation.
Circulation	Excellent for disturbed energies.
Concentration	Use with yellow.
Confidence	Helps with confidence.
Digestive Disorders	Increases appetite.
Depression	Wear color to bring joy.
Emotion	Use with indigo to heal and recharge the etheric aura.
Energy Drain	Use with red.
Epilepsy	Use in environment-walls, décor.
Exhaustion	Revitalizes
Eyeballs	Use if eyes have bluish tinge instead of white.
Fingers (cold)	Wear mittens/gloves in bright orange.
Gallstones	Helps relieve long-time bitter resentment which leads to gall stones.
Gas (Intestinal)	Relieves

Color Me Healthy Wealthy and Wise

Orange is Excellent for:	Comments (continued)
Headaches	Relieves
Hiccups	Relieves gas and aids digestion.
Impurities	Clears
Intestines	Stimulates
Kidneys	Helps inflammation.
Lungs	Strengthens
Learning Disabilities	Creative concentration.
Lethargic	Wear/ have in environment.
Mental Debility	Sharpens mental facilities.
Mucous	Releases
Nails (ridged)	Results from phlegm in system.
Pancreas	Strengthens
Parkinson's	Rooted in fear, anger not expressed, hardening in arteries at the base of brain, lose balance - use in combination with green and indigo.
Posture (poor)	Will help alignment of spine.
Prostate Gland	Associated with sacral chakra.
Rheumatic Conditions	Use with blue and indigo.
Pulse Rate	Helps to raise pulse rate.
Sinuses	Helps ease congestion and mucous.
Spleen	Strengthens
Soft Teeth	Associated with calcium.
Toes (cold)	Wear bright orange socks.
Ulcers	Relieves
Urine	Improves flow.
Weak and Shaky	Use orange over solar plexus and blue over throat.

Yellow is Excellent for:	Comments
Addictive Problems	Aides in self-control and self-worth.
Adrenalin	Releases physical need to do something.
Allergies	Helps in countering hypersensitivity to environment.
Arthritis	Loosens and eliminates calcium and lime deposits in joints.
Bile	Promotes flow.
Boils and Abscesses	Use with violet.
Catarrh	Use with Indigo.
Colds	Associated with Vitamin C and sunshine.
Cold (Congestion)	Boil grapefruit with skins. This liquor has natural quinine. Mix this liquor half and half with water and drink.
Constipation	Massage colon area with yellow or lemon as it helps cleanse and release stools.
Cysts (Fatty)	Use yellow and green.
Deafness	Use yellow light over ears with eyes covered. Combine with indigo.
Diabetes and Hypoglycemia	Focus on pancreas.
Digestion	For good digestion, gas, food allergies, liver, use all yellow foods to aid digestion, i.e. lemon.
Diuretic	Affects bowels, bladder, good for cleansing and toning system; if bowels, bladder overactive, use indigo.
Ears (Congested)	Use yellow scarf around neck .
Emotional issues	Use in conjunction with pink and blue to calm and stabilize.
Eyes	Rinse with solarized yellow water.
Gallstones	This turns stones into a fatty substance, which leaves the body anywhere between 12 and 50 hours. 1/2 C. lemon juice & 2 C. olive oil. Every 15 minutes, drink 1/4 C. oil and then 1 Tbsp. lemon juice over a period of 2 hours. Must take full dose, i.e. all lemon juice and all olive oil.
Hair	Yellow solarized water adds gloss.
Hay fever	A Lemon juice fast clears allergies.

COLOR ME HEALTHY WEALTHY AND WISE

Yellow is Excellent for:	Comments (continued)
Heartburn	Drink lemon water/alkaline water.
Herpes	Use with violet.
Irritability	Use with green, pink and blue.
Liver	Yellow acts to stimulate liver functions.
Lymph Glands	Stimulates
Memory	Sharpens it - move from yellow to green.
Melancholia	Sunny yellow brings happiness and joy.
M.S.	Results from dead cell tissue in the nervous system. Use yellow with indigo.
Muscles	Stimulates
Nerves	Relaxes - good for Nervous Exhaustion. Strengthens nerves. If Irritable nerves, use green, pink and blue instead. If Emotional Nerves, use soft pink and blue.
Nerves and Bones	Builds
Noises in head	Drink lemon solarized water/lemon; use with Indigo.
Overwork	Helps mental fatigue.
Prostate	Assists if caused through fixed mind, ideas.
Piles	Improved digestion helps elimination.
Purifier for whole system	
Scars	Helps skin, blemishes.
Skin Grafts	Visualize yellow to accept new skin and improve graft; green to heal.
Spirits	Raises spirits.
Stimulates	All bodily functions - Spleen, Pancreas, Kidney. Increases Vital fluid flow within body (chemical processes in vibrational form). Stimulates cells and tissues. Use solarized water.
Urine	Improves flow.
Weight Corrective	Promotes essential rhythms within body; weight gain often occurs when people have generally lost their internal rhythms.
Worms	Cleanser

Green is Excellent for:	Comments
Anger	To transmute anger, red for passion with green for compassion.
Anxiety	Calms and balances.
Asthma	Breathe into lungs to calm and improve airflow.
Balance	The impulse to move on, when the patient is suddenly getting better, becoming more balanced.
Biliousness	Tonifies liver and gall bladder.
Blood Clots	Helps to dissolve.
Blood Pressure	Controls - has an equalizing effect, like a tranquilizer.
Cancer Growths	Send green light, which induces calmness.
Cancer Tumors	Use green and pink especially if no green in aura.
Emotional Problems	Green relaxes and balances.
Headaches	Green relaxes and balances.
Hay Fever	Helps balance system and reduce histamine response.
Heart	Helpful in all problems of the heart. When Heart chakra open, the compassion, empathy and understanding results in healing. When Heart center hurts, green takes down emotional walls to let out the grief-not self-pity. We all need more green! Many today with Heart issues have not been able to link with Soul - green relaxes fear and is very sensitive. Heart is the first center to degenerate when taking strong coffee/Tea/Smoke. Many bottled-up emotions need released - upheavals have strong effect on heart area, as well as drugs. We must express ourselves. Heart Center should be silent and peaceful. Green helps release congestion from heart - lifts fear in heart and de-stresses. Aids our etheric body by loosening and equalizing heart center.

Color Me Healthy Wealthy and Wise

Green is Excellent for: Comments (continued)

Jaundice	Use with Yellow on Sacral and Solar Plexus Centers.
Liver Conditions	Use green foods.
Memory	Stimulates
Muscles and Tissues	Builds
Nervous Disorders	Green is great for all nervous disorders and tonic for nervous system. With a Nervous Breakdown, wear emerald scarf. Put one on the back of chair & rest head on it. Go into Nature, breathe in and out. Connect with fir, eucalyptus and cypress trees.
Nervous System	Soothes - gives self-control along with blue.
Nervous Strain	Brings peace.
Sedative	Green is considered a sedative to help one relax and sleep.
Shock	Calms and balances.
Strokes	Helps restore body's balance.
TB	Aids in airflow and energy to Dorsal (back chest of body) area.
Tension	Relieves
Thought Forms	Visualize soft rose with green which breaks thought forms. Emerald green is the harmonizer of thought forms.
Toxic Wastes and Viruses	Helps expel.
Ulcers	Heals both internal and varicose ulcers on legs.

Blue is Excellent for:	**Comments**
Asthma	Attacks can be aborted with blue light through stained glass. Use blue and violet plus turquoise light.
Blood Pressure	Blue reduces; red increases blood pressure.
Breath	Cleanses
Bruising	Reduces
Burns	Cools
Cancer	Liver cancer patient will need cool blue and green energy to act as sedative limiting over-activity of liver cells.
Children's Ailments	Good for all kinds of children's health challenges.
Deafness	Hearing is Throat Chakra issue.
Diarrhea	Soothes intestines.
Earache	Use blue energy compress.
Ear	Helps middle ear infections.
Etheric	Heals etheric aura body.
Fever	Cools system, excellent for any inflammation, fever.
Goiter	Helps by focusing blue light on throat for 3/4 hour. Also can use blue oil plus coconut oil and vitamin E in oil. Rub over throat area.
Hair	Blue solarized water strengthens brittle hair.
Headaches	Reduces all headaches, including migraines.
Heart	Slows down pulse rate.
Insomnia	Use with indigo.
Immune System	Combine with turquoise to tonify.
Irritation	Soothes
Liver	Cleanses

Color Me Healthy Wealthy and Wise

Blue is Excellent for:	Comments (continued)
Mental Depression	Relaxes mind, gives harmony.
Nervous Issues	Use with green.
Nosebleed	Slows blood flow.
Painkiller	Contraindicated if high blood pressure present.
Palpitations	Use with Heart Chakra and Emerald to calm.
Periodic Pains	Calms
Pregnancy	Blue is good during pregnancy and good for baby since the Mother's aura shows blue in pregnancy.
Rheumatism	Releases inflammation in acute flare-ups only.
Scars	Use blue oil with Vitamin E.
Sciatica	Balances lower Root Chakra by calming.
Sore Throats	Use blue lozenges for simple soreness.
Shock/Trauma	Think blue and green.
Sleep	Eases into sleep.
Sunstroke	With green, cools system.
Swelling	Excellent for swelling especially if bruised too.
Tension	Relaxes mind, gives harmony.
Thyroid	Calms over-active thyroid.
Throat	Eases any issues with throat. To replenish throat, first stop talking. Put tongue up or down out of action. Feel the color blue spread out as the sky and sea radiate. Let the throat open.
Tonsillitis	Helps with laryngitis as well.
Tranquilliser	Ultimate calming color.
Ulcers	Use with green.
Varicose Veins	Use with green.

Indigo is Excellent for:	Comments
Asthma	Some forms of asthma and digestion are caused by a deep fear factor and psychic anxiety. **Indigo** handles the psychic level, helping other levels as well.
Anti-Bacterial/Parasitical	Use with **violet**.
Bleeding	Slows internal bleeding and hemorrhages.
Boils	Anti-bacterial
Acute Bronchitis	Use with **orange**.
Bruises	Apply raw onion (especially if before bruise comes out) plus **indigo** oil or deep **violet** oil.
Burns	Cools
Calms	In emergency
Cataracts	A third-eye chakra challenge.
Cell Tissues	Recharges
Convulsions	Use sparingly to calm.
Cools System	Use with **blue**.
Deafness	A third-eye chakra challenge.
Eczema	Calms skin.
Eye Issues	May manifest if cannot see situations in life clearly.
Facial Paralysis	A third-eye chakra challenge.
Fears	Stabilizes
Goiter	Helps
New Growth and Tissue	Promotes
Grieving	Helps connect with spirit.
Headaches	Use with **blue**.
Heart	In heart attack, use on forehead to stabilize.
Inflammatory conditions	Cools
Insomnia	A third-eye chakra challenge. Brings peaceful dreams.
Intestines	Relieves congestion.

Color Me Healthy Wealthy and Wise

Indigo is Excellent for:	Comments (continued)
Lung Infections	Use with orange.
Memories	Neutralizes negative memories.
Mental Complaints	Positive effect on mental challenges.
Migraine	Use with blue.
M.S.	Use with yellow.
Nervousness	Soothes
Nosebleeds	Stops nose bleeds.
Over active	Calms
Pain	Lessens pain.
Parathyroid	Stimulates
Psychotics	Works to clear mind.
Rejection	Helps to stabilize.
Rheumatism	Calms and cools acute stages.
Sedative	Lessens pain.
Schizophrenia	Dis-ease of imbalance in 6th chakra - very spiritually tuned in childhood and repressed.
Sinuses	A third-eye chakra challenge.
Slipped Discs	Linked to skeleton system.
Soothing	
Swellings	Eases
Thyroid	Depresses over-active.
Tiredness	Helps connect with inner wisdom and strength.
Tissue	Promotes new growth.
Tonsillitis	Use with blue for all throat issues.
Ulcers	Use with green.
Spider Veins	Use with green.
Varicose Veins	Use with green.

Violet is Excellent for:	**Comments**
Appetites	Improves depressed appetites.
Bladder	Helps bring calm to issues & challenges.
Anti-bacterial	UV light used to remove bacteria from water.
Blood	Nourishes blood in upper brain region. Purifies blood along with yellow.
Bone	Good for bone growth.
Calms	Use in combination with green, blue or indigo.
Cancer	Ultra violet aids in coping.
Coccyx	Energy condensed here and stuck creates an itch, violet will release and recharge all chakras.
Concussion	A crown chakra challenge.
Cowardly	To regain confidence use with yellow.
Cramps	For baby's cramps use blue and violet solarized water.
Cystitis	Anti-bacterial to fight urinary tract infections.
Energy Depletion	Use violet and indigo.
Pre-exams	Use also for stage fright, event presentations.
Headaches	Eye and nervous headaches, back of head pain.
Heart	Depresses and slows down pulse.
High-strung	Calms and desensitizes.
Inflammatory Conditions	Cools
Insomnia	Use with indigo to bring peace and promote sleep.

Color Me Healthy Wealthy and Wise

Violet is Excellent for:	Comments (continued)
Irritability	Controls and calms.
Kidney	Use with **orange**.
Lungs and TB	Use with **orange** and **green**.
Meningitis	Use with **green**.
Mental and nervous	Calms emotional disturbances if excessive.
Migraines	Use on top of head - out of spirituality - depressed.
Nerves	Soothes inflammation of nervous system.
Neck	Use on back of neck, effective on whole body via pituitary.
Over-activity	All conditions of over-activity of glands and organs.
Potassium/sodium	Maintains balance in body.
Protects	From negative/non-growth energy.
Rheumatism	Use with **indigo**.
Scalp and Hair	Use in disorders of the scalp.
Sedates	Slightly sedating to heart, muscles, lymph glands.
Subdues	Disburses over-activity. Must have outlet fro energy.
Slows Down	Everything - rhythm of heart, breathing, thoughts.
Slimming	Aid - good for some.
Spleen	Stimulates along with **orange**.
Terminal Illness	Helps make peace and forgiveness.
Upliftment	Spiritual - especially for divorce, gives much strength - links humankind to spiritual levels.
Violence	Reduces

Notes:

15

Gemstone Correspondences And Guides

*Chakra Gemstone Correspondence Guide
*Gemstone Corresponding Energies

Chakra Gemstone Correspondences Guide

Root Chakra	Sacral Chakra	Solar Plexus Chakra	Heart Chakra
Black Tourmaline (S)	Carnelian (S)	Amazonite (S)	Amazonite (S)
Bloodstone (Q)	Coral (Og)	Amber (Og)	Apophyllite (S)
Boji Stones- C	Hematite (1)	Citrine (Q)	Aventurine (Q)
Garnet (S)	Orange Calcite (3)	Clear Quartz (Q)	Azurite (6)
Hematite (1)	Rainbow Moonstone (S)	Golden Calcite (3)	Bloodstone (S)
Jasper (S)	Sunstone (S)	Rainbow Fluorite (5)	Chlorite in Quartz (Q)
Obsidian (S)	Tiger's Eye Agate (Q)	Rutilated Quartz (Q)	Chrysocolla (S)
River Rock-C	Zincite (4)	Tiger's Eye Agate (Q)	Dioptase (S)
Ruby (2)		Topaz (S)	Green Tourmaline (S)
Septarian Nodule-C			Kunzite (S)
Smoky Quartz (Q)			Malachite (6)
			Moldavite (S)
			Peridot (S)
			Rhodochrosite (7)
			Rose Quartz (Q)
			Watermelon Tourmaline (S)

Key— Mineral Composition

Q=Quartz family (1) Iron Oxide

S=Silicate (2) Aluminum Oxide

C=Concretion (3) Calcium Carbonate

Og=Organic (4) Zinc Oxide

Chakra Gemstone Correspondences Guide

Throat Chakra	Third Eye Chakra	Crown Chakra
Angelite (8)	Azurite (6)	Amethyst (Q)
Aventurine (Q)	Charoite (S)	Chlorite in Quartz (Q)
Celestite (Blue) (9)	Clear Quartz (Q)	Clear Quartz (Q)
Kyanite (S)	Herkimer Diamond (Q)	Fluorite (5)
Larimar (S)	Lapis Lazuli (S)	Lepidolite (S)
Magnesite (10)	Malachite (6)	Moonstone (S)
Rose Quartz (Q)	Rainbow Fluorite (5)	Rainbow Moonstone (S)
Smokey Quartz (Q)	Sodalite (S)	Selenite (12)
Sodalite (S)	Sugilite (S)	Watermelon Tourmaline (S)
Blue Tourmaline (S)	Cat's eye Tourmaline (S)	Zircon (S)
Turquoise (11)	Zircon (S)	

Key— Mineral Composition

(5) Calcium Fluoride (9) Strontium Sulfite

(6) Copper Carbonate (10) Magnesium Carbonate

(7) Mag. Iron Zinc (11) Copper/aluminum

(8) Lead Sulfite (12) Calcium Sulfate

Gemstone Corresponding Energies

Agate - Blue Laced	Peace, inspiration, grace; helps Solar Plexus and Throat Chakras; soothes nerves; stone of happiness; connects Third Eye and Crown chakras; gives inspiration and grace
Agate - Fire	Influences entire endocrine system and memory
Amazonite	Aligns Heart and Solar Plexus Chakras; Communication and expression
Amber	Fossilized resin; helps Throat and Solar Plexus Chakras; removes emotional and physical pain; soothing, healing, peaceful and calming.
Apache Tears	Obsidian with white flecks; releases grief, emotional pain, anger; Grounds the Root Chakra; helps lower body issues.
Amethyst	Crown Chakra; enhances spiritual awareness and encourages inner vision; protective gem that absorbs and transforms negativity; draws energy within for self-healing and illumination; calms; relaxes physical body; emits purifying energy; restores harmony and balance; gives compassion, more understanding.
Aventurine	Heart Chakra; cleanses etheric, emotional, and mental bodies; helps ally anxiety and fear; promotes positive attitude for life; promotes Thymus gland health; opens both Heart and Throat Chakras
Azurite	Heart Chakra; balances liver and thymus gland; assists with depression, anxiety, emotional imbalance; cleanses subconscious mind when place over Third Eye; penetrates negative mental states; helps with physical detoxification.

Color Me Healthy Wealthy and Wise

	Gemstone Corresponding Energies
Calcite - Green	**Heart** Chakra; Used in childbirth to turn baby; good for candida; helps manipulate tissue.
Calcite - Honey/Golden	**Solar Plexus** Chakra; Assists cramps in abdominal area.
Carnelian	**Sacral** Chakra; encourages contact with nature spirits; aids access to memories of other lifetimes; helps us to dream great dreams; heals spleen and pancreas; draws warmth to you; energizes Creativity.
Celestite	**Throat** Chakra; Brings truth to your authentic voice.
Citrine	**Solar Plexus** Chakra; balances **Solar Plexus** Chakra; cultivates clarity, warmth, and sense of self; solar energy; assists in digestive imbalances; helps alleviate pain; aids digestions by relaxing organs; frees breath through diaphragm; helps asthma; relieves tension headaches; wear around neck for self-confidence and courage; dispels anxiety and negativity; Points and clusters assists in alleviating pain; Attracts prosperity.
Chrysocolla	**Heart** Chakra; Peace stone - message of peace to planet; Feminine issues for balancing hormones; tranquil and powerful energies; patience, kindness, tolerance, compassion and humility; activates any chakra; calms nerves; helps with sore throats.
Crystal - seed	Releases blocks
Fluorite	Balances your entire energetic system.
Fluorite - Rainbow	**Solar Plexus** and **Third Eye** Chakras; Enables communicating your personal power and setting personal boundaries; Connects the intuition of the **Third Eye** Chakra and awareness of self of **Solar Plexus** Chakra; counters depression and disillusionment; breaks up unwanted energies & seeds for positive intentions.

Gemstone Corresponding Energies

Garnet	Root Chakra; aids tissue healing and regeneration; assists in transitions and life changes; speeds any physical healing and manifesting; brings comfort for physical loss; helps to appreciate the physical; creates rapid energy, heat, and warmth; works with heart, blood circulations; very grounding; use with survival issues; stimulates.
Hematite	Sacral Chakra; activates Sacral Chakra; assists all blood disorders relating to iron; elevates low self-esteem; Balances magnetic field in body.
Herkimer Diamond	Third Eye Chakra; enhances dreams; cuts through blockages, finds toxins; creates very intense and high frequency; natural double terminated quartz crystal found in New York USA.
Jade	Heart Chakra; may be too intense an energy for heart especially if healing.
Jasper	Root Chakra; Encourages abundance and helps heal fears or wounds from poverty and deprivation; assists in power and empowerment; as water element, promotes sensitivity and sense of direction.
Labradorite	Balances upper chakras: Throat, Third Eye, Crown
Lapis	Third Eye Chakra; power stone, heals the mental deeply within the mind; enhances communication; enhances hypnosis when placed over Third Eye; helps mind and throat; best is from Afghanistan.
Malachite	Third Eye Chakra; Grounds and dissolves negative energies; circulates more energy; enhances mental clarity; Works with azurite for strengthening energy field; draws out negatives; strengthens Third Eye inner vision; helps open and circulate more chakra energy.

Gemstone Corresponding Energies

Gemstone	Energies
Obsidian	Root Chakra; Grounding; awareness of life cycles of birth/death/rebirth; improves stamina and natural wisdom.
Peridot	Heart Chakra; opens, cleanses and activates the Heart Chakra; counters the effects of negative emotions; relieves depression; connects with higher self; attracts wealth, abundance and financial success; Aligns subtle energies; brings good loving feeling.
Pyrite	Often found in lapis; good for mind.
Quartz - Clear	Universal Energy; can be used with any chakra to amplify and balance energy; gives energy to entire aura; attracts all seven rainbow colors to physical body; attracts life force energy to disharmonious areas; balances emotional extremes; aligns Third Eye and Solar Plexus Chakras.
Quartz - Rose	Heart Chakra; Used with most Chakras to transform and integrate energy; heart energy of unconditional love; self-nurturing; connects with guardian angels; soothes and opens heart; eases trauma of past sorrow; balances emotions of four upper Chakras; initiates self-love, healing, and compassion; creates peaceful, calming feeling; relieves stress and disharmony; balances Throat Chakra; Helps kidneys and adrenals.
Quartz - Smokey	Root Chakra; Grounding; helps alleviate emotions of grief and loss; Throat Chakra; draws energy to physical; protects against negative vibrations and depression; good for healers; Beneficial for channels as protects against lower octave energies.
Rainbow Moonstone	Sacral and Crown Chakra; assists in transitions; helps to move from retributive to redemptive karma; brings peace and harmony; aligns energy in vertebrae; harmonizes abdomen, pancreas, and pituitary.
Rhodochrosite	Heart Chakra: Cleans Solar Plexus; integrate physical and spiritual energies; helps eyesight; helps physical and emotional healing; works with malachite to allow more spiritual energy in.

Gemstone Corresponding Energies

Ruby	A master gem for the **Heart** chakra; same properties as Garnet for **Root** Chakra.
Snowcaps	Also known as Milky Quartz; Crystals enhance immune system and give great energy; promotes greater understanding of emotions.
Sodalite	**Third Eye** Chakra; **Throat** Chakra; heals breaches in communications; unites logical and spiritual; assists in logic, rationality, efficiency and making decisions; stimulates thought; truth in communication; balances left and right brain activity; assists in cleaning lymphatic system; balances thyroid gland.
Sugilite (lavulite)	Helps **Third Eye** Chakra; links mind with physical; establishes conscious control over mental faculties; shows why you created physical imbalances and what lessons are involved; pressure release valve for mental stresses; best for sensitive people; stone of high awareness.
Tabis	**Root Chakra**: Flat with rounded edges, powerful to hold one in each hand; balances energy and links with higher self.
Tiger's Eye agate	**Sacral** Chakra; quiets nerves; aids sleep; helps muscle cramps and asthma; centers energy; cleanses adrenals; Combines gold of sun, brown of Earth; good for **Sacral**/**Solar Plexus** Chakras.
Topaz	**Solar Plexus** Chakra; helps abdominal issues; found deep in the earth.

Gemstone Corresponding Energies

Tourmaline	Queen of gemstones; surpasses quartz in both piezoelectric and thermoelectric properties for conducting energy.
Tourmaline - Black	Balances **Root** Chakra: Tunes into higher octave energies to maintain spiritual consciousness; deflector of negative energies; helps restructure cellular memory and allow more freedom of sexual responsibility and expression.
Tourmaline - Cat's Eye	Balances **Third Eye** Chakra.
Tourmaline - Green	**Heart** Chakra; Used for purifying and balancing the inner body organs and nervous system; places mental, spiritual and higher self into perfect alignment; helps relieve fatigue and rejuvenate the body, cells and blood patterns; looking at it will help to ease eyestrain.
Tourmaline - Green blue to light blue	Balances **Throat** Chakra; Used in vocal communications; worn around neck allows truthful expression and clarity in messages; relaxes nervous stress and reduces high fevers and sore throats.
Tourmaline - Pink	Calming
Tourmaline - Rubellite	Excellent for opening love awareness; loving oneself more.
Tourmaline - Watermelon	**Heart** Chakra; assists in compassion and transformation; tolerance and flexibility; promotes inner honesty and insight; maintains the flexibility to keep the **Heart** Chakra healthy; aids in the deeper understanding of spiritual surrender; relaxing and balancing; absorbs and radiates love; queen of gemstones; very calming; both piezoelectric and thermoelectric; opens **Crown** Chakra; aligns all auric bodies and Chakras; its energies radiates to wearer as well as those exposed to its view.

Gemstone Corresponding Energies

Turquoise	**Throat** Chakra; facilitates communications with all that is natural; aids in communication with nature spirits and higher self; Master Healer of all Chakras; Strengthens entire body; re-aligns all Chakras; protects against environmental pollutants; calms, steadies; provides peace and harmony.
Zircon	Balances **Third Eye** and **Crown** Chakras; balances pineal and pituitary glands.

Metals

Copper	Great conductor of electricity; balances body's polarities; element = water; **Heart** Chakra; connects physical and astral bodies; aligns a gem stone's individual energy field; amplifies and transmits thought and healing energy; combats fatigue, lethargy, restlessness; helps in acceptance of self; strengthens pineal and pituitary glands; aligns first through 5th (Root through Throat) Chakras.
Brass	An alloy of Copper & Zinc; similar properties as copper.
Gold	Activates and balances energy; opens and activates **Third Eye** and **Crown** Chakra; balances **Heart** Chakra; clears negativity; activates positive energies of minerals and gemstones; solar energy; symbolizes wealth and happiness; Master Healer.
Silver	Mirrors soul; strengthens connection between physical and astral bodies; balances intuitive and psychic energies; calming; reflective; moon energy.